Gardening 101

Gardening

Learn how to plan, plant, and maintain a garden

101

The Best of Martha Stewart Living

Copyright © 2000
Martha
Stewart
Living
Omnimedia
LLC
11 West
42nd Street,
New York, NY
10036
www.marthastewart.com

Originally published in
book form by Martha Stewart
Living Omnimedia LLC in 2000.
Published simultaneously by
Clarkson N. Potter, Inc.,
Oxmoor House, Inc., and
Leisure Arts.

A portion of this work
was previously published in
MARTHA STEWART LIVING.

Manufactured in the
United States of America.

Library of Congress Cataloging
in Publication Data is available
upon request.
ISBN 0-8487-1935-2 (hardcover)
0-8487-1971-9 (paperback)

Text
Thomas Christopher

Editors
Margaret Roach and Douglas Brenner

Art Director
Linda Kocur

Additional Text
James A. Bielaczyc

Assistant Art Director
Jill Groeber

Copy Editor
Debra Puchalla

Design Production
Duane Stapp

Contents

Preface: Choosing Your Garden

Any garden begins with a decision: What style of landscape best suits you? Of course, a garden's design should also reflect the circumstances of the site—a sun-drenched acre of Southwestern desert demands treatment that's very different from what a cool and cloudy woodland lot in the Pacific Northwest might call for. Still, above all else, a garden is your sanctuary, and if well designed, the result should fit you as neatly as a well-cut suit.

As with clothing, achieving a good fit in the garden involves careful shopping. Before running down to the nursery, before pushing a spade into the soil, you should consider what style of garden makes you comfortable. Visiting gardens can help you establish this; bring a notebook and record the settings in which you feel most at home. Note, too, the conditions that those particular plantings enjoy: the amount of sunlight the plants receive, the soil conditions, and the topography of the site. Be sure to ask gardeners whose places you admire about the amount of time and care they give to their landscapes. Keep in mind that a small but well-kept garden is generally much more attractive than an expansive but neglected one.

Bring your observations home, and then reinterpret them to suit your circumstances. A garden should enhance your lifestyle and the activities with which you fill your leisure time. In addition, it should harmonize with the style of your house, since garden and structure must work together if either is to look its best. Actually, a well-designed garden plays an essential role in mediating between architecture and the surrounding landscape, giving a house that look of truly belonging.

A cottage-garden tangle of old-fashioned flowers, for example, extends the nostalgic charm of a restored farmhouse into the surrounding landscape. That stately Victorian is a lovely relic of a more decorous age; it may want color, but color organized into neatly defined beds. A modernist house of bold, geometrical shapes, on the other hand, would look harsh in either of those settings—it sits more easily in a landscape of crisp, simple lines.

You may find, however, that you enjoy the drama you achieve by planting against type. For example, the right-angled space of an entryway might seem to call for a formal treatment. Fill it with an explosion of unruly tropical foliage, though, and the approach to the front door becomes extraordinarily romantic.

Whatever the overall style of the garden, it should include diverse moods. Efficiency will probably dictate a clean, somewhat formal configuration in the area that you set aside for outdoor entertaining. But the bench where you sit and read a book on a summer afternoon will be far more appealing if given a softer, less disciplined setting. Regardless of your goal, the following chapters will guide you to the plants, the tools, and the techniques that will make that special place a reality.

Introduction: Before You Start

Right Plant, Right Place

It's easy to fall in love with a plant. But before you rush to install that shrub or tree, flower or ground cover in your garden, pause to consider what sort of tenant it is going to make. If the plant won't thrive in your garden, or if it is likely to thrive too well and become a weed, or if it just can't get along with its neighbors, then admire the plant by all means, but in someone else's garden.

Matching the Plant to the Site

The following are essential factors that determine the types of plants that will flourish on your site.

• **Sun and shade:** In general, plants described as requiring "full sun" need at least six hours of exposure to direct sunlight daily. "Part sun" or "semi-shade" plants flourish where periods of direct sunlight alternate with periods of shade, or where the sunlight is filtered by an intermittent canopy of branches or a trellis overhead. "Full shade" describes a spot where direct sunlight never penetrates, due to shadows cast by dense evergreens or solid man-made structures, such as a high wall or a porch roof.

• **Rainfall:** You can compensate for drought with irrigation, but gardening will be much easier (and more economical) if you landscape with plants that are satisfied with the natural rainfall you receive. In areas of low rainfall, the local water utility often can furnish lists of such adapted plants. Check,

too, with your local extension agent; you'll find the extension office listed among the state or county offices in your telephone book under county or cooperative extension service.

• **Hardiness zones:** The United States Department of Agriculture has divided the entire country into eleven "hardiness zones," each of which experiences a different degree of winter cold. Nurserymen conventionally use the USDA's zone map to specify which plants are "hardy" in their regions; that is, which plants will survive local winters. Use our reproduction of the hardiness map, on page 128, to determine your zone. Note that a plant described as "hardy to" zone 6 or zone 5, for example, will generally survive not only in the zone specified but also in those with higher numbers.

• **Drainage:** This is the soil's ability to absorb moisture and let excess water drain away. You can test soil drainage by digging a hole a foot deep and a foot across. Fill the hole with water, and time how long it takes the water to drain away; two to three hours after the hole has emptied, refill it, and again time the interval it takes for it to empty. Then calculate the rate of drainage by dividing the total depth of the water (24 inches) by the total number of hours it took for the hole to

Opposite: Snapdragons (Antirrhinum majus) display the profusion of colorful blooms that make these annuals equally welcome in the ornamental flower bed and the cutting garden. Grow snapdragons in full sun in well-drained soil that is rich in organic matter.

empty two times. An average rate of an inch of water lost per hour marks a "well-drained" soil, which is best for most garden plants. A substantially faster rate is typical of a "sharply drained" soil, one that dries out quickly, and unless enriched with water-retaining compost, is suitable mainly for drought-tolerant plants. A drainage rate markedly slower than an inch per hour indicates poorly drained soil, which will probably drown the roots of all but bog-loving plants.

Green Architecture

Without rhythm or melody, a succession of notes is just noise, not music, and in the same fashion, a garden without structure is nothing but a menagerie of plants. Structure is the backbone that connects the different elements of the garden, organizing the plantings into related units. It may be as simple as a curving path of stepping-stones set in gravel, the line that separates and defines two opposing flower beds in an informal cottage garden. Or the structure may be more elaborate—as in the geometric patterns of low hedges or meticulously framed raised beds within a formal herb garden. In either case, though, structure is the essential organizer.

The most natural way to begin structuring your plantings is to think like an ecologist, and visualize your landscape in three "stories." There is the garden floor—the perennials, turf, and other earth-hugging plants that spread out

at ground level—and above this is the canopy of tree branches. In between is the understory, the shrubs and smaller trees that serve as partitions to divide and define spaces within your garden.

Because your house is, typically, the focus of the garden, the landscape's structure should reflect some aspect of the house's architecture. The axis of a central hall, for instance, may continue out the door and down the garden's central path. The vistas you arrange can provide views for the principal windows. A particular kind of brick or stone, even a certain color, used on the exterior of the house can be repeated in garden paving, fences, or walls to unify the landscape.

In fact, many gardeners take an architectural approach to structuring the garden as a whole, using hedges or fences to subdivide the garden into separate areas or "rooms," each with its own function and character. Hedges and other barriers, both living and man-made, can provide enclosure, security, and privacy, but they also serve as transitions. Step through the gate, an arbor, or a gap in the hedge, and you leave behind one experience—the romantic tangle of a meadow garden, say—and emerge into something entirely different, such as the utilitarian order of a kitchen garden.

Similarly, you should use paths not only to provide access to different areas of the garden (paths should be as direct as possible and wide enough for a wheelbarrow to pass) but also to control the sequence in which visitors enjoy the garden's experiences. Like a well-told story, a piece of land and a grouping of plants can be organized to inspire a sense of mystery, wonder, adventure, and surprise.

A plan drawn to scale on paper is a useful way to begin working out ideas. You'll get a far better sense of where your design is going, though, if you use a tape measure, stakes, and string to translate your plan from paper to garden, and then lash together bamboo stakes to mock-up fencing, arbors, and other structural elements. After living with the mock-ups for a while, you'll know if you've gotten the proportions and placement right. If you haven't, it takes only minutes to move or reshape the bamboo constructions and try something else.

Common Planting Mistakes
• **Underestimating size** Before installing any plant in your garden, check the size it will reach at maturity, and make sure the planting spot can accommodate that. For example, a fast-growing, expansive tree or

Often, the garden architecture that looks most at home in the landscape is a structure that invites plants to climb it or to cluster at its feet. Opposite: A rustic cedar arbor supports Japanese wisteria while moss cushions the fern-lined stone pathway below.

shrub planted under a window will soon block the view; beside a path, it will block traffic. You can contain many trees and shrubs with pruning, but the continual clipping this requires is a headache.

- **Garden thugs** Some plants, such as Japanese honeysuckle, purple loosestrife, and many bamboos, though attractive, spread aggressively and are likely to turn into troublesome weeds. The character of a plant may vary regionally—often, a plant that is well behaved in the colder or drier part of its range may be a thug where the climate is more benign. Your local extension service is a good source of information about such problem plants.

- **Pairing incompatible plants** Setting plants with different needs side by side ensures that one, or both, will not thrive. For example, plant English lavender, which thrives in dryish, nutrient-poor soils, amid moisture-craving, fertilizer-hungry New Guinea impatiens and you have guaranteed failure.

- **Catering to pests** Some otherwise desirable plants are so attractive to pests and diseases that allowing them into the garden is an invitation to infestation. English boxwood, for example, which is prone to attack by parasitic nematodes, makes a poor shrub in Southern areas where such parasites are endemic in the soil. Save yourself work by sticking to plants that your nurseryman or extension agent recommends as pest- and disease-resistant.

Developing a Personal Palette

Too many gardeners are uneasy about their ability to work effectively with color. Design jargon such as "saturation," "tones," and "color values" baffle many otherwise confident people, leaving them feeling that matching plant to plant is a craft only experts should attempt. Yet most of us manage to put together a coordinated outfit when we dress in the morning, and composing an attractive garden picture really isn't much more difficult.

Everybody has favorite colors, and it makes sense to start with those when you assemble your personal garden palette; after all, the primary goal of gardening is to please yourself. Use a favorite hue as your main theme, then identify the range of colors that harmonize with it. One quick and painless way to test flower and plant combinations is to find potted specimens at the garden center and set them side by side right there—before lugging them to the checkout counter. If you have

identified plants that you want in a friend's garden, ask to cut some flowers and foliage, and see if they make an attractive arrangement in a vase.

The best test of any color scheme, though, is a field test with annuals. How will scarlet and silver look together? Plant a window box of scarlet sage and dusty miller, and you'll know whether that combination works in a matter of weeks. If it doesn't, pull up those annuals, and try something else. An additional advantage of annuals is that their extended season of bloom practically guarantees that the different-colored flowers will actually appear at the same time. Perennial catalogs are misleading in that respect: The blue iris pictured on page 16 might look ravishing next to a bright pink dahlia, but, outside of catalog photographs, the two flowers will never appear at the same time.

Keep in mind that colors are simply reflected light, and that the quality of the sunlight in your garden will have an influence on the effect of flower colors. The brilliance of a Southwestern landscape washes out "cool" pastels; "hot" colors such as yellows, oranges, and reds stand up to that harsh light. Pastels are more at home in the soft light of the North, especially in an area of dappled sun or shade.

Opposite: In the soft sunlight filtered through a high canopy of trees, a woodland garden's "understory" plantings and ground covers display a rich, subtly varied palette of greens. Left: Heirloom tomatoes come in many appealing colors aside from "tomato red."

Time of day also changes the quality of the sunlight, and if you tend to be out in the garden at a certain hour, plant accordingly. Whites, silvers, and pale colors show up well in the gentle radiance of a morning garden, and blues glow at twilight, but in the glare of high noon you need the bolder, more stalwart reds, yellows, and oranges. Don't waste precious space on color effects that no one will be present to appreciate at their peak.

Certain colors affect your perception of the garden in very specific ways. Blues, for instance, seem to recede from the eye, and so masses of blue flowers can make a small space seem larger. Reds, by contrast, jump out at the eye, and red flowers will make a large space seem more intimate. Because yellows and chartreuse have a sun-drenched look, they are useful for bringing an illusion of sunshine and warmth to cool, shady areas.

The bulk of any plant is always its foliage; therefore, the prevalent color in your garden will nearly always be green. Of course, there are many plants, such as coleus and the variegated hostas, whose leaves furnish a variety of other colors. Yet even "plain" green-foliage plants offer tremendous variety, ranging as they do from dark blue-greens like that of the holly *Ilex* x *meserveae* 'Blue Prince' to pale silvery greens like those of lamb's ear *(Stachys byzantina)*. Between the main seasons of bloom in a sunny area, and year round in a shade or woodland garden, the subtler contrasts you create with foliage will constitute your garden's main source of interest.

Because flowers play a minor role in the kitchen garden, foliage color is especially important there. Think color as well as flavor when ordering seeds—many herbs, in particular, such as the purple basils and sages or golden thyme, have leaves that are as appetizing to the eye as to the tongue. And colorful vegetables and fruits can beguile you long before they reach the table.

When planning color schemes, keep seasonal flowering schedules in mind. Opposite: Late-blooming New England asters, Salvia 'Indigo Spires,' and Zinnia angustifolia in fall. Left: Spring-blooming iris, poppies, and alliums in Martha's Connecticut garden.

Starting From Scratch

The success of any garden depends on preliminaries. The care with which the gardener prepares the soil and the plants—even the care with which he or she selects the tools—is the foundation on which any garden is built. Skimp on the foundation and the garden will always be a ramshackle affair; the most beautiful flower, if its roots are stuffed into poor soil, will never amount to much. • If done well, preparation is painstaking work, but the time you invest in this way will be returned many times over in the labor you save in the years to come. A well-tended healthy garden is naturally resistant to pests, diseases, and drought. As simple a precaution as clearing a bed of perennial-weed roots before you plant will save you endless hours of weed pulling and hoeing later. A garden that is easy to maintain doesn't happen by accident; it is the product of planning ahead.

Whether Martha is planting a shrub from the nursery, such as this balled-and-burlapped lilac, or adding fallen leaves to her compost bin, she knows that an attractive, healthy garden must be created from the ground up. Improving the texture and fertility of the soil is fundamental to success throughout the seasons, wherever you garden and no matter what you want to grow.

Most of the time, a "new" garden isn't really new. Instead, it's your transformation of an existing landscape, inherited from the house's previous owner, or perhaps a rethinking of your own earlier effort. In either case, before you start planting, pause to identify—and eliminate—the annoying time-wasters that every garden seems to accumulate.

• **Remove odd corners of lawn.**
If you can't mow it without stopping and backing up, turn that turf into ground cover or mulch. By smoothing jagged contours, you can reduce weekly mowing time by as much as half.

• **Consolidate plantings.**
Isolated shrubs and islets of flowers dotted amid a lawn not only increase mowing time, they complicate tasks such as watering and fertilization. One large bed is far easier to care for than several little ones.

• **Maximize accessibility.**
Keep plantings that require regular watering close to a spigot or sprinkler system so you won't have to drag out a hose. Make sure that the toolshed and compost heap are out of view and yet easy to reach when you need a tool or want to dump a basketful of weeds.

• **Discard liabilities.**
Old, established plantings can be an asset, but a tree that's shedding limbs is a hazard, and an overgrown shrub in obvious decline is merely depressing. It's simpler and cheaper to clear away such nuisances before you have surrounded them with new plantings.

Nurturing the Soil

It's difficult to overemphasize the importance of the soil in gardening: It is the source of thirteen of the sixteen elements that are considered essential to plants. In fact, the dictionary defines soil as a medium that supports plant life. That's why a good gardener is, above all else, a conscientious soil builder. And the time to start this task is before the first seed is lowered into the ground.

Soil can be amended (improved) physically or chemically. Physical soil amenders include organic materials, such as compost and manure, and texture-changing inorganic materials, such as sand. Chemical amenders include lime, which changes the pH (acidity or alkalinity) of the soil, as well as the packaged fertilizers that contain nitrogen, phosphorus, and potassium.

While chemical fertilizers are easy to use, no amount of chemical tinkering

can substitute for physically enhancing the soil's texture and organic content. A good-textured soil loaded with decayed organic matter, such as compost, is the best growing medium for most plants. Unfortunately, most soils weigh in at a sorry 5 percent or less of organic content.

But before adding anything to the soil, get an accurate reading on its condition by submitting soil samples for testing by the local county extension agent (you'll find the office number listed in your telephone book among the county or state offices) or a private soil-testing laboratory. The testing process can evaluate your soil's texture by measuring its organic content, its pH, and how much of the necessary nutrients it contains. This isn't a major expense: Typically, a simple pH test at the extension service costs about $10, and a combined nutrient and textural analysis less than $20. However, it is important to start with truly representative samples; the procedure for taking those is outlined on page 22.

Soil is made up of three kinds of particles: sand, silt, and clay. The relative proportion of these in your soil determines not only how the soil will handle water and how workable and aerated it is but also offers clues about its fertility. An accurate reading of soil composition comes from the

One of the many ways to amend your soil is the application of nutrient-rich rock powders. Here, in springtime, rock powders are distributed evenly with an ordinary garden spreader. Depending on the chemistry of your particular soil, powders can be applied either singly or as a blend.

laboratory test, but you can make a preliminary assessment with a simple hands-on technique that literally gets you in touch with the earth.

Just rub a small amount of soil between your thumb and forefinger. Does it feel gritty and neither sticky nor moldable? If so, your soil is sandy, a common phenomenon in coastal regions. Silt, widespread in the Midwest, feels more like flour or talcum powder and is only slightly moldable. Clay is very moldable and feels sticky when moist. The higher the clay content, the longer the ribbons you can make by rolling moist soil between your palms or on a flat surface. Slightly moisten a handful of the soil, squeeze it into a ball, and drop it onto a paved surface; if it doesn't splat or shatter, but merely cracks, it's loam, a balanced combination of clay, silt, and sand that is the most desirable garden soil.

The qualities of loam are what you are aiming for when you amend garden soil. Depending on what you start with, how much of what material or materials you add will vary. However, decomposed organic matter—compost—is the best all-around cure. That's because it can do many jobs.

Depending on the materials from which it was made, compost can add small but significant amounts of nutrients to the soil, and it helps to retain the nutrients released by fertilizers, keeping them from washing out. Compost also bonds with mineral particles to open pores within the soil, making room for the air and water needed by roots. This is especially beneficial to heavy clay soils, which are particularly common in the Southern states. Because of their density, clay soils drain poorly and commonly lack the air that roots require, because the space between particles is too small. An addition of organic matter, such as compost, is the best corrective. Yet compost also greatly improves sandy soils, which are fast-draining often to a fault, and typically drought-prone. Mixed in with the sand, compost particles act like tiny sponges, absorbing water that would otherwise run away.

You can make compost at home, acquire it from the leaf-composting program of your local municipality, or buy it bagged or in bulk from a garden center. What matters most is that you use a lot. Incorporating a foot-thick layer of compost into the top foot and a half of a new bed isn't

- **Compost**

  Made by decomposing organic wastes such as leaves or kitchen vegetable scraps, as well as manure, compost is the best all-purpose soil amendment. A good alternative to aged manure is the bagged dehydrated kind.

- **Gypsum**

  Like lime, gypsum opens pores in heavy soils, but because, unlike lime, it has no effect on the pH, it is recommended for use on alkaline soils. Gypsum also reduces soil's sodium content, which is often injuriously high in arid regions.

- **Lime**

  If soil is excessively acidic, a common condition in many parts the Eastern states and the Pacific Northwest, lime may be added to raise the pH. Lime also helps to open up pores in heavy clay soils.

- **Sawdust**

  By-products such as finely ground bark or wood shavings boost organic content, but they steal nitrogen from the soil while decomposing. Compensate by increasing fertilization.

- **Sharp builder's sand**

  This lightens clay-heavy soils. Sand, which is inorganic, lacks the nutrient- and water-retaining qualities of compost. However, because it does not decompose, the lightening effect of sand is permanent.

- **Sphagnum peat**

  Often called peat moss, this is good for lightening soil but has almost no nutritive value and breaks down quickly.

- **Sulfur**

  This element is used to increase acidity and reduce the pH of overly alkaline soils, which are common in the arid West and Midwest.

overdoing it; about half that much should also be worked in each subsequent year, preferably in fall so time and winter weather can mellow the ingredients. In spots where perennial plantings prevent more disturbance, lightly hand-cultivate a couple of inches around plants each year.

Caring for the soil is an ongoing process. Test the pH every spring with one of the do-it-yourself kits available at garden centers. Never dig or walk in wet soil, as that will compress it. Don't overtill; you're not aiming for a fine powder but a grainy consistency. And don't leave the soil naked: Cover beds and borders and the cultivated areas around the bases of trees or shrubs with a protective blanket a couple of inches deep of some organic mulch such as shredded bark or cocoa hulls.

Soil Testing

Collecting a soil sample is a simple process, but one that must be carried out with care. For if the sample you collect doesn't accurately reflect the condition of your soil, the results of the test will be worthless. Worse than worthless, actually, as they may lead you to waste time and money adding amendments to your soil that it doesn't need. Rather than improving it, you may make it worse.

Because the soil composition can, and usually does, vary widely even

Top: It is easy to take samples for a comprehensive soil analysis, which will help you find out which vital nutrients are abundant or lacking. For accurate results, use a clean trowel to dig several soil samples from the garden area to be tested, put them in a stainless-steel or enameled bowl, mix well with a trowel or spoon, and place the mixture in a plastic bag. Above: Your local county extension agent can supply a soil-analysis kit, including forms to fill out and submit with the samples.

within a single backyard, it's best to test a sample from each general area to be cultivated, such as the vegetable garden, the cutting garden, or a perennial border. The difference in soil from area to area may be considerable. Next to the foundation of a house, for instance, the soil will often be alkaline, from lime leaching out of the concrete, even in notoriously acid-soil areas such as the Northeast.

Collecting Soil Samples

Select several spots within one planting area. Scrape any plant growth or leaf litter off the soil's surface at each spot and, with a stainless-steel trowel or a large stainless-steel spoon, dig a hole 6 inches deep. Take care not to touch the sample with soft steel, galvanized or brass tools, or with your bare skin, since this may contaminate soil and distort the test results.

Cut a uniform vertical slice off the side wall of each hole. Make sure the slice runs all the way from the soil surface to each hole's bottom. Mix the slices together in a clean plastic or stainless-steel container; when evenly mixed, take from this blend the sample you'll submit for testing, and pack it in a clean plastic bag.

Label each soil specimen with its place of origin: "vegetable garden," "front flower bed," and so forth. If you take the sample in for analysis yourself, the pH-test results will probably be immediate. It will take a few days (or even weeks, if samples must be mailed away) to complete the other tests. The reports you receive will tell you the condition of your soil in each location and how to improve it.

Compost

Composting should begin with a bin. A freestanding heap produces compost just as well, but because it's unsightly, the temptation is to hide it in the remotest corner of the yard. That means extra hauling, both to and fro. A well-constructed bin, by contrast, looks at home in some businesslike area of the yard, such as the cutting garden—right where you need it most.

A bin should be large enough to retain the heat generated by decay and yet not so large that air cannot penetrate its interior. Both of these conditions are requirements for efficient decomposition, as the microorganisms most effective at this process flourish only at high temperatures and in the presence of oxygen. The ideal measurements for a bin are a width, length, and depth of 3 to 4 feet. Making the walls of the bin out of wire mesh also helps air get to the decomposers, as does lining the bin's bottom with a porous layer of twigs 6 inches deep.

Theoretically, any organic material is compostable, but in practice it's best to keep all meat scraps and dairy products out of your bin, as these might attract scavenging animals. Barnyard manure or even a pet rabbit's droppings make a rich compost, but those of a pet dog or cat are likely to carry parasites and diseases. Also avoid adding to your heap any materials that have been treated with pesticides or weed killers.

Like you, your bin needs a balanced diet. Too much wet green material, such as fresh grass clippings or fresh manure, may cause the heap to collapse into a foul-smelling, oxygen-deprived mass; stuff it with dry leaves or cornstalks, and decomposition will slow to a crawl. The best recipe calls for two parts brown and dry materials to one part green and juicy. Chop or shred large items, such as Halloween pumpkins, and mix the different kinds of debris thoroughly with a garden fork.

Water the bin periodically to keep its contents moist (but not soaking wet). A soil thermometer, available at most garden centers, is useful for monitoring the rate of decay. The temperature within the bin should rise as high as 160 degrees; when the temperature drops, turn the bin's contents to introduce more air. When the compost has cooled and subsided into a crumbly dark-brown substance like coffee grounds, it's ready to use.

Far left: A sturdy homemade bin has ½-inch hardware screen stapled to a 4-foot-square frame of 2-by-4s. Eye hooks hold corners together. Center: Heavy-duty plastic composters are available at many hardware stores and garden centers. Near left: A 4-foot-tall cylinder of 1-inch chicken wire makes a simple yet effective composting bin.

making compost

Composting is more than a matter of heaping up gardening castoffs and kitchen scraps willy-nilly. The secret lies in achieving a balance between woody matter (such as twigs and branches), an excellent source of carbon, and "green matter" (e.g., fresh leaves and discarded vegetables), which is rich in nitrogen. Given the right mix, the microbes that exist wherever there is organic debris will quickly get to work digesting the contents of the pile. As decomposition proceeds, the pile will heat up; on a cold winter day, you can actually see a pile give off steam. Once the original mass of raw material "cooks" down to rich, blackish-brown compost, a pile can shrink to as little as one-quarter of its original volume.

1 Start with a 3- to 4-inch layer of branches as a base (this large, woody material will take longer to decompose than leaves, stems, fruit, and other soft debris). The next layer should include lots of green matter, such as grass clippings, deadheaded flowers, vegetable plants that have passed their prime, and kitchen refuse (avoid meats, fats, and dairy products, which will attract unwanted animals to the bin).

2 Keep the bin's contents moist (but not sopping wet), because much of the water present in succulent foliage and other plant matter is lost through evaporation. And since regular air circulation is key to composting (microbes that break down the debris use up large amounts of oxygen, which must be replaced), turn or toss the compost as it begins to settle, approximately every 5 to 10 days.

3 Use a compost thermometer to measure the temperature inside the bin. Most essential microbial action occurs at high temperatures, as hot as 160 degrees or more in a large bin. This heat also serves to kill off weed seeds and plant pathogens that may be present in garden debris. If the temperature falls below 90 degrees, it is time to turn the pile again.

4 Pass the finished compost through 1/2-inch hardware screen stapled to a frame to remove small stones and chunks of stubborn woody materials. It takes about 4 to 6 months to compost an entire 4-by-4-by-4-foot pile down to usable "brown gold."

Beneficial Rock Powders

The typical synthetic fertilizer acts like a drug: It furnishes an immediate rush of nutrients but soon washes out, leaving the soil even more depleted and the plant in need of another fix. Rock powders, on the other hand, are a natural source of essential minerals. Mined from natural deposits, they are slower than synthetics to release their nutrients, and so longer lasting in their effect. Because they feed the soil and plants at a more uniform rate, they promote stronger, healthier growth. These sturdier plants are naturally resistant to pests and diseases and better able to cope with drought. Gardens nourished with rock powders have also been shown to produce sweeter, more flavorful fruits and vegetables.

Apply powders with an ordinary garden spreader in the spring, and work them into the soil with a tiller or fork; or apply them to the soil surface in the fall, and let the earth absorb them gradually over the winter.

Dealing with Problem Soils

Sometimes the good earth we acquire with our house is not so good. The soil may be so rocky and shallow that plant roots can't gain a foothold, or it may be a clay so dense that rainwater pools on the surface and every sticky shovelful must be scraped off by hand. In the Southwest, caliche, a concrete-like layer of mineral deposits, all too often lurks just below the surface. That region has no monopoly on such hardpan, however, for subsurface layers of compacted, virtually impenetrable silts and clays are present locally throughout the United States.

The natural impulse is to dig down in an attempt to improve the soil. Often, though, the more effective, and far easier, solution is to "graft" better soil onto the garden's surface by constructing a raised bed. This is an area where the existing soil has been amended and piled up, or where a good, organic-enriched loam has been hauled in, to create a plateau as much as a foot high that offers superior growing conditions. In its simplest form a raised bed is self-supporting, a heap of soil that has been raked to a level surface. Most gardeners, however, prefer to enclose raised beds in a frame of timbers or low brick or stone walls. Such enclosure not only

Rock powders mined from natural deposits release their nutrients more slowly, and with longer-lasting results, than synthetic soil additives. A soil test should be your guide in determining whether your garden will benefit from these ground minerals.

a rock powder sampler

- **Greensand**

  A form of glauconite, an iron-potassium silicate originating in marine deposits. Greensand stiffens sandy soils and loosens dense clays. Especially recommended for rose growers because greensand imparts brighter color to the flowers. A typical application is 50 pounds per 1,000 square feet, with new applications made every five years. Take care not to overuse—too much greensand creates a harmful imbalance in the soil.

- **Limestone**

  Available at garden centers, but usually in the form of dolomitic limestone, which is high in magnesium, low in calcium, and needed only for magnesium-poor soil. More commonly, soils are deficient in calcium, which plants require for optimum growth, and "high-calcium" limestone is a richer source of that mineral. Apply according to your soil's acidity; on a soil with a pH of 5.5, most garden plants benefit from an application of 50 pounds of limestone per 1,000 square feet. One application every five to six years is sufficient for most gardens. Do not use limestone if you're growing acid-loving plants such as blueberries.

- **Rock dust**

  Either quarry by-products or alluvial deposits, rock dusts vary in character, but those sold by organic-gardening suppliers are packed with minerals and elements such as potassium, which stimulates root growth and strengthens stems. Application rates vary with rock-dust type.

- **Rock phosphate**

  A source of trace minerals as well as phosphorus, an essential element in plant germination, cell division, and mineral absorption. A typical application is 20 pounds per 1,000 square feet of garden the first year and 10 pounds annually thereafter.

stabilizes the beds' edges; it gives them a neater, more attractive look.

Because the soil within raised beds has been thoroughly dug and in general heavily amended, it typically offers a nearly ideal texture and high nutrient value. As a result, it promotes better plant growth and higher yields of flowers, vegetables, and fruits. This superior soil also allows more intensive planting. Raised-bed vegetable gardeners, for example, arrange their plants not in rows but instead in grid or hexagonal

patterns, so that every bit of soil is used. When plants are set closer together, spaced so that they touch at the leaf tips when mature, they shade the soil below, reducing moisture loss, blocking the soil compaction caused by raindrops, and thwarting weeds—a self-mulching phenomenon.

Raised beds are ready extra early in the spring, a particular benefit in cold zones where the soil in the beds tends to be workable before the open ground thaws and drains. Finally,

Sometimes the easiest way to deal with problem soil is to bury the problem. Raised beds can be built on top of ground that is depleted or hard to dig, and then filled with amended soil. Fencing wards off pests.

raised beds significantly reduce the need for tilling: Unlike conventional flat rows, which are compacted as the gardener walks between them, a raised bed need never be stepped on, since it is tended by leaning across from one side or another.

building a raised bed

1 Select a level, sunny site. Mark off the bed layout with corner stakes and string. The bed may be as long as the site permits. If you intend to frame the bed with wood, you'll reduce waste if you make the length equal to some multiple of standard lumber lengths. The bed's width should be such that you can reach anywhere inside it without stepping in.

2 Cut the turf along the perimeter with an edging tool. Using a pick, shovel, and garden fork, loosen and remove clods of turf for composting. Loosen underlying soil as deeply as possible, preferably 12 to 18 inches. A pick or a large crowbar may be needed in rocky areas.

3 If the walls are to be longer than the individual boards, butt two pieces together, and secure with a short third board nailed to the inside surface. Cut the short board an inch or two narrower than the main boards, and position it below their top edges: When the bed is filled with soil the top of the short board won't show.

4 Construct the frame as a bottomless box, using pressure-treated lumber to protect against decay (buy lumber several months ahead of time and leave it exposed to the weather, so undesirable chemicals can leach out). Environmentally concerned gardeners can substitute naturally rot-resistant woods such as cedar or locust, or may treat pine or fir by painting it with Donnos, a rot-proofing liquid made from natural ingredients such as citrus oils and tree resins.

5 Cut the boards for the ends of the bed, then assemble the frame by nailing its walls together at the corners in simple butt joints. To keep beds longer than 10 feet long from wobbling, reinforce them with cross braces made of 2-by-8s. Position braces inside the bed, and nail them from the outside. Set the top edge of the braces below the top edges of the bed so that they, too, will be hidden by the soil.

6 Cover the paths between the beds with landscape fabric, a synthetic material that allows water to drain but prevents weed growth. The fabric must be tucked beneath the beds, which can be lifted with a pry bar. (Wood-chip mulch will be added later.)

7 Two of the beds are about to be pried up and lowered onto the fabric. Once the beds are in position, slightly below soil grade for stability, secure them with interior corner posts. These are made from pressure-treated 2-by-2s cut on an angle at one end, and long enough to be driven into the ground below the frost line.

8 Knock the posts into place with a sledgehammer until they're an inch or two below the top of the wall; then nail them to the box. The bed will then be ready to be filled with topsoil, compost, and other organic matter, and the paths ready to be covered in mulch.

gardener's latin

They are hard to pronounce and hard to remember, and when you do utter a Latin plant name, the neighbors raise an eyebrow, but that's too bad. To garden seriously, you can't escape botanical nomenclature. Besides, if you do learn how to decipher all of those Latin names, you will find them full of clues as to how different plants should be used in the garden, the kind of care each plant requires, and even when and how specific plants bloom.

Common names are easier but fatally imprecise. A rose of Sharon, say, isn't a rose at all, but instead a hibiscus, a shrub that doesn't even belong to the rose family. Nor is it related to rock roses (*Cistus*) or sun roses (*Helianthemum*), both in the Cistaceae family.

Besides, the latinized names aren't so hard to deconstruct. Every plant gets two. The first, always capitalized, is the "generic epithet"—the name of the plant's genus, which is, botanically speaking, its immediate family. A rose, for example, a real rose, always has the genus name "*Rosa*." It is the second name, the uncapitalized "specific epithet" that identifies the plant's species, its personal identity. And usually, it is in this name that you find the clues to its needs and nature. Take *Rosa palustris*; "palustris" is Latin for "of the marsh" or "marsh-loving," and if you understand that, you'll know that this plant, alone among roses, thrives in poorly drained soils.

In checking through the following glossary, you'll notice alternative endings included in parentheses after each Latin word. One of the more confusing aspects of the Latin language is that names take a gender—male, female, or neuter (don't ask)—and that the gender of the specific epithet must be the same as that of the generic one.

Glossary of Botanical Names

Here are some Latin species names that can help make the processes of reading catalogs and labels, and choosing a plant and siting it correctly, a little easier.

natural habitat

alpestris (-e): from lower mountains below the timber line

alpinus (-a, -um): from high mountains above the timber line; best for the rock garden

aquaticus (-a, -um): aquatic; plant in the water garden

arenarius (-a, -um): native to sandy soils

campestris (-e): a plant of fields and open land

pratensis (-e): a plant that grows in meadows

maritimus (-a, -um): a plant native to the seaside

palustris (-e): marsh-loving; a good bet for wet soils

saxatilis (-e): native to rocky sites

sylvaticus (-a, -um), sylvestris: native to woodlands

umbrosus (-a, -um): native to shady areas

size and pattern of growth

columnaris (-e): column-shaped

fastigiatus (-a, -um): narrow and upright in profile

globularis (-e): ball-shaped

grandis (-e): large, as in *grandiflorus* (large-flowered) and *grandifolius* (large-leaved)

nanus (-a, -um): dwarf

procumbens: growing along the ground

pyramidalis (-e): pyramid-shaped

repens: a creeping plant

season of principal display, usually season of flowering

aestivalis (-e): summer

autumnalis (-e): autumn

hyemalis (-e): winter

vernalis (-e): spring

flower or leaf color

albus (-a, -um): white

argenteus (-a, -um): silver

aurantiacus (-a, -um): orange

aureus (-a, -um): gold

azureus (-a, -um): sky blue; *caeruleus (-a, -um)* is somewhat darker; *cyaneus (-a, -um)* is darker yet

flavus (-a, -um): pale yellow

luteus (-a, -um): yellow

purpureus (-a, -um): purple

roseus (-a, -um): rose-colored, pink

ruber (rubra, rubrum): red

sempervirens: always green; i.e., evergreen

variegatus (-a, -um): variegated; foliage splashed with various colors

viridis (-e): green

fragrance

aromaticus (-a, -um): aromatic

foetidus (-a, -um): stinking

fragrans: fragrant

inodorus (-a, -um): having no smell

odoratus (-a, -um): sweet-smelling

pungens: pungent

geographic name: specific epithets often indicate the plant's place of origin

amazonicus: suggests that the plant originated in the Amazon River basin (the wise gardener will not expect it to survive in Minneapolis, Minnesota)

virginianus: a good bet for gardens in the Middle Atlantic states; will never embarrass the American native-plants enthusiast

Propagation

If you buy all of your plants in containers at the garden center, or order them through the mail, you are not only paying top price, you are limiting yourself to the specimens some nurseryman judges to be most saleable. That's why discriminating gardeners become experts at home propagation.

Essentially, propagation is the process of making new plants from old. To do this, you may plant seeds, divide a large clump of stems and roots into two or more smaller clumps, or take a cutting—a piece of a leaf or stem—and persuade it to grow roots and develop into a complete plant. Mastering these simple techniques opens up new worlds of plants that simply are not sold at most nurseries.

The local garden center, for example, may offer two or three kinds of tomato seedlings. But start your own from seed, and you have access to hundreds of cultivars from around the world: red, yellow, even "black" tomatoes, tomatoes sweet and tart, tomatoes ideal for sauce or sun-drying. You'll never find a catalog listing for the old-time rosebush you admired in your grandmother's garden—who knows what its name is? If you know how to root a cutting, though, you can easily make the heirloom your own. Skillful propagators' gardens yield a steady harvest of new plants as the existing ones reach a size sufficient for division, so that either filling gaps or expanding the garden is cost-free.

For the beginning gardener as well as the veteran, no project is more hopeful or rewarding than raising plants from seed. Here, seedlings started indoors, under fluorescent light, in early springtime are ready to move outside to their place in the garden.

Starting from Seed

Watching seedlings emerge in early spring is one of the most exciting moments of the gardening year. Observe a few precautions and this process is close to foolproof, too.

Some types of seeds, particularly vegetables, grow best when "direct sown"—that is, when planted directly into the garden soil. But frost-sensitive annual flowers and vegetables such as tomatoes that require a long, warm growing season must be started indoors throughout most of North America. It's often best to start perennials in containers as well, as that allows you to control temperature, light intensity, moisture levels, and

starting seeds

other aspects of their environment.

Whatever you plant, start with good-quality fresh seed. The viability of seeds—the reliability of their germination—declines as they age, so it's important to buy seeds packed for the current growing season. You'll find the year in which the seeds were packed printed on the packet. Viability also drops if the seeds are stored improperly and exposed to heat and humidity, which is why it's best to avoid the racks of bargain seeds you may find in the local hardware store or supermarket.

Clay or plastic pots and plastic cell packs all work well for starting seeds indoors and may be reused if you sterilize them after each use by washing them and then soaking them in a solution of ten parts water to one part chlorine bleach. Peat

that's been dug up from the garden, as this may contain bacteria and fungi that will attack emerging seedlings. Avoid such problems by using one of the naturally sterile peat-based seed-starting mixes you'll find at garden centers.

Seed packets commonly recommend starting the seeds they contain a certain number of weeks before "the last frost," the average date in spring when temperatures may be expected to remain above 32 degrees. To determine when this is in your area, check with your public library or call the local extension agent.

Finally, you'll achieve far more success with indoor sowings if you start them under fluorescent lights. A pair of double-tube, four-foot fixtures provide sufficient candlepower, and if you equip each with one cool white and

Division

Division provides a quick, straight-forward way to increase your stock of multistemmed perennial flowers and ornamental grasses, bulbs, even those shrubs such as spireas and Siberian dogwoods that sucker, sending new shoots up from the ground around their periphery. This form of propagation offers instant gratification: In a matter of minutes, one plant becomes two or even more, depending on the size of the original. Besides multiplying your plants, this procedure typically renews their vigor. As a plant exhausts the soil around its roots, its crowded tangle of stems bears fewer and fewer blossoms; by transplanting the fragments to fresh soil with room to spread, you return them to vigorous growth and healthy bloom.

Start your own plants from seed, and you'll have access to hundreds of varieties that aren't available at the local garden center.

pots and peat pellets are good only for a single use, because you leave them around the roots of the seedling when you transplant it into the garden (the roots grow through the peat). However, peat containers have the advantage of being naturally sterile, and a seed packet may specify their use if the plant you are starting has sensitive roots that are easily damaged during transplanting.

Whatever kind of containers you decide to use, do not fill them with soil

one warm white tube, they'll provide a nearly ideal balance of light. Suspend the fixtures so that their tubes rest 2 inches above the surface of the seed-starting mix. At this level, the heat from the tubes warms the seed-starting mix just enough to encourage germination. As the seedlings grow, raise the lights. Before germination leave the lights burning around the clock; after germination, reduce the period of lighting to 16 hours a day.

In general, divide plants when they are dormant. For hardy perennials, grasses, and shrubs this means early spring or fall. In northern climates, spring division is usually best, because it gives plants several months to re-establish themselves before facing the stress of winter. In the South, where winters are mild and summer heat and drought are the greater threat, fall division is safer. Divide hardy bulbs in summertime, after the foliage has yellowed and died back to the ground.

giving seeds a start

1 Pour the seed-starting mix into a pail or dishpan, and moisten it with hot water, adding a cup at a time until mix is evenly moist but not wet, like a wrung-out sponge.

2 Cover the drainage holes in clay or plastic pots with a single thickness of newspaper so that the seed-starting mix won't leak out; peat pots and pellets and cell packs don't need this treatment. Then fill your pots, trays, or packs right up to the top of the lip with the moistened mix. Brush off any excess. Tamp down the remaining mix in the container with the bottom of an identical pot; with cell packs, use your fingertips. The surface of the mix should be firm and level, 1/2 inch below the top of the container's lip.

3 To avoid disturbing the seeds, water containers from the bottom by standing them in 1 inch of water inside a dishpan. Leave the containers in the water until the moisture has risen to the surface of the seed-starting mix. The surface will darken and feel slightly damp to a fingertip.

4 Unless seed-packet instructions specify leaving the seeds uncovered, cover them with additional seed-starting mix to a depth equal to three times their diameter. A seed that measures 1/16 inch across, for example, should be buried to a depth of 3/16 inch. Don't worry about being exact; seeds don't mind being buried a bit too shallow or too deep. Do not cover really fine seeds; the sand with which you should mix them before sowing provides the coverage they need.

5 Hardy seedlings can be raised under artificial light. Double-tube fluorescent fixtures from a hardware store, with one "cool" tube and one "warm" tube in each fixture, provide the full light spectrum necessary for healthy seedling growth. Fixtures can be attached to the undersides of shelves above seedlings or hung from the ceiling. Suspend lamps from hooks with chain; adjust links to raise fixtures as seedlings grow, keeping lights about an inch or two above the seedlings throughout their development. Seedlings need 12 to 16 hours of light daily.

6 Mark plastic, wooden, or metal labels to record plant names and the days seeds were sown. When transplanting seedlings into their new containers, always hold by the first set of leaves. Grasping the stem can bruise and injure the tender plant.

7 To transplant seedlings from a community pot, carefully slide the entire clustered root mass out of the pot and cradle it in one hand. Then turn the root mass so that the seedlings stand upright and hold it about 8 to 10 inches above a work surface. Let the root mass drop onto the work surface; the impact will help separate the "community" into individual rooted seedlings without tearing the delicate root fibers. Lift each seedling by its leaves and plant it into its own cell pack.

dividing a plant

Division is a frugal, satisfying way to get more from what you already have—and to share the wealth with gardening friends. It is also often the best way to rejuvenate a mature though lackluster perennial. Some plants, such as German iris, whose tubers or roots naturally tend to rise out of the soil, actually need to be divided and replanted periodically. But no matter why you're dividing, *when* you do it is critical. Spring is a good time, and fall even better. Then, with an entire season's growth visible above ground, it's easy to determine the full extent of the root system you need to unearth and separate. Besides, moderately cool autumn days provide ideal conditions for divided plants to recover from surgery and put out new roots.

1 The day before you dig up a perennial that spreads by runners, or stolons, close to the soil surface, water the plant well to keep roots and soil together. With a trowel, dig around the entire root mass, about 1/2 inch beyond the plant's outermost foliage. Go deep to avoid damaging the roots. Carefully lift the plant out onto a tarp laid near the bed.

2 Because this plant (a potentilla) has long, loosely entwined roots, it can easily be pulled apart by hand. If any roots refuse to snap or break neatly, don't tear them; instead, cut with pruning shears. Torn or frayed tissue heals slowly and offers an entry point for soil-borne pathogens. If you begin with a plant that measures about 10 to 12 inches in diameter, separate it into no more than two segments. Smaller divisions will need several seasons to fill out and mature.

3 For perennials with tough, massive roots or rhizomes, such as this astilbe, you may need a spade or small shovel to dig up the whole plant (again, water well before digging). Use a Japanese weeding knife or other sturdy blade to divide the plant in two. Try to cut cleanly, in a single smooth motion.

4 Because tough, dense roots are quite vigorous, you can divide the halves again, to yield four substantial chunks. It's best to plant these divisions as soon as they're made. If you must wait, wrap them in damp newspapers, place them in a plastic bag, seal it, and refrigerate it for no longer than 2 days.

Because rhododendrons and evergreen azaleas (both, in fact, members of the genus Rhododendron) can be propagated by softwood cuttings, it is possible for the home gardener to expand and share a collection of these shrubs without purchasing additional plants. Any time from midsummer to fall, take cuttings from the most recent growth at the tip of a branch.

Shrubs from Softwood Cuttings

Is there a gardener anywhere who hasn't rooted a cutting of a coleus or geranium? Yet for some reason, most of us do not think to apply the same technique to deciduous shrubs and vines. The truth is, if you can root one, you can, with a little extra care, root the other. And propagating shrubs and vines in this manner can provide special prizes: a rosebush grown from the long stem of a wedding bouquet blossom, for instance, or a living memento of a favorite fragrant lilac

left behind in some former garden. Aside from roses and lilacs, this method of propagation is effective for a broad range of species, including viburnum, ceanothus, wisteria, honeysuckle, and trumpet vine.

Softwood cuttings are lengths of stem taken, as the name indicates, from the soft new growth. The best time to make such cuttings is in late spring or early summer, just after the flush of spring growth ends and the stems start to turn woody. When exactly does this transition occur? That

depends on the local climate, but the stems are ready if they are still soft enough to cut almost effortlessly yet are crisp enough to snap rather than crush when you bend them. Make sure, too, to harvest stems for cuttings in early morning, before they are wilted by the heat of the day.

Snip the stems from the bushes with a sharp pair of bypass pruning shears whose scissorlike blades cut cleanly and without crushing. Use the shears, if they are very sharp, or a sharp knife to divide the stems into cuttings; the

rooting softwood cuttings

1 Scissors-type bypass pruning shears are the best tools for harvesting stems (use finer floral shears to cut especially delicate stems). A clean, sterilized pair will give a neat cut and prevent the transfer of disease. A cleanly cut stem roots faster and more easily. Take cuttings early in the day when temperatures are cool.

2 Buds are closely spaced on this willow. Cut ½ inch below a node with a pruner or floral shears. Strip leaves away from the cutting. Leaves left intact on the stem and buried in rooting medium will rot, fostering disease and impeding root growth.

3 After stripping foliage from the lower part of the cutting, slice larger leaves in half. The cutting's end is then dipped into a rooting-hormone powder, which initiates root development. Select a hormone that contains a fungicide in its formula. Fungicides inhibit plant diseases and the rotting of cuttings. Lightly dip cutting's end into the hormone powder.

4 Prepunch holes with a pencil so the rooting-hormone powder won't be rubbed off when the cutting is planted. Fill the tray with a rooting medium, which should include perlite or coarse sand for good drainage. Be sure to pack the medium densely into the cells of the tray, and moisten thoroughly. This will eliminate air pockets that inhibit rooting.

5 Pack rooting medium around the cutting to ensure good contact between cutting and medium. Use your finger or a pencil to firm each cutting into place; try to center each cutting in its cell for uniform root development. If the cutting can be lifted out of the medium with a slight tug, it needs to be replanted more securely.

6 A fine shower of water prepares cuttings for the sweat box. The water source can be a watering can with a rose attachment, a mister bottle, or a hose with a misting adapter on the end. Moisture is crucial to success in rooting, but it's touchy to regulate. Too much moisture can lead to rot; too little will prevent root formation. The best measurement for gauging moisture content is to lift the tray: As the rooting medium dries, the tray will feel lighter.

7 The time it takes for cuttings to develop roots depends upon the kind of plant. To propagate a large new plant as quickly as possible, place several rooted cuttings into a single container, as shown here.

disposable snap-blade razor knives sold at art-supply stores are an inexpensive and effective tool for this job. Cut the stems into lengths that include at least three nodes each; a node is the point from which a leaf sprouts. Cuttings of compact growers such as cotoneaster and barberry may include as many as ten nodes, but as a rule, cuttings should be no more than 4 to 6 inches long. Trim the bottom of each cutting ½ inch below the lowest node, and then snip off the leaves

the active ingredient—are best. To apply, dump a little of the powder on a saucer. Dip the base of each cutting into water and then into the powder, then tap the cutting sharply to shake off any excess. When all the cuttings have been treated, throw out any leftover powder; returning it to the container will contaminate the contents and shorten their shelf life.

To root the cuttings, put them in a "sweat box," a homemade miniature greenhouse. Fashion this from a tray

keep them evenly moist. Generally, softwood cuttings root within three to four weeks, though some take as many as eight. Test by tugging gently on a leaf. If the cutting resists, it's rooted; if it starts to pull free, it needs more time, so replant it.

When cuttings have rooted, transplant them to 4-inch pots filled with a standard potting mix. Leave them under the plastic for a few days, then move to a sheltered spot outdoors. Water regularly, and feed with half-

Grow a rosebush from a long stem in a wedding bouquet, or propagate a new lilac with a cutting from a favorite shrub left behind in a former garden.

from all but the two uppermost nodes. If the remaining leaves are expansive, like those of viburnum, trim each leaf back by half, to reduce moisture loss through the foliage.

Treat each cutting's base with rooting-hormone powder. This product is a mixture of talc and some synthetic version of the chemicals that plants themselves use to trigger root production. Powders are manufactured in a range of concentrations; for softwood cuttings, the least concentrated forms—those containing .2 percent or less of

of plastic cell packs like those used for starting seedlings. Fill the cells with a mixture of equal parts sphagnum peat and perlite or coarse, clean sand (sold as "sharp" sand by masonry-supply centers). Moisten the mix, and firm it down with your fingertips. Drop the cuttings, one to a cell, into holes prepunched with a pencil, pack the mix back in around the cuttings' bases, and water well with a gentle spray. Once you've filled the tray, cover it with a tent made from a dry cleaner's plastic bag. Hoops made from wire coat hangers will hold the plastic up and off the cuttings.

Check your trays weekly. Remove any fallen leaves, and water cuttings to

strength soluble fertilizer every second week until late summer. When cool weather causes the infant shrubs to drop their leaves, move the pots into a cold frame or a frost-free garage with temperatures between 29 and 42 degrees. The next spring, transplant them into a nursery bed, a fertile but inconspicuous patch of earth where youngsters can grow until they are ready to take their place in the garden.

- **Handle:**

  If wooden, it should be straight-grained and free of knots or flaws. Ash makes strong, light handles and is used for the best tools; hickory is second best, just as strong but heavier. Avoid tools with painted handles; the paint was probably applied to hide poor-quality, flawed wood. Fiberglass, steel, and aluminum are stronger but less shock-absorbent than wood.

- **Blade or Head:**

  In the best tools, the blade or head typically ends in a seamless socket that fits cuplike around the handle's end. In cheaper tools, the blade or head usually ends in a pointed tang that has been driven into the handle's end; a ringlike ferule binds the handle end, to keep the tang in place.

- **Metalwork:**

  Seams and welds should be even and smooth; cutting edges should be sharp and free of nicks and burrs. Forging, whereby red- or white-hot steel is rolled over dies to form the shape, results in a stronger tool. Forged steel is about twice as expensive as stamped or laser-cut steel. Stainless steel is rust resistant and thus easier to maintain than high-carbon steel, which will rust unless wiped dry and oiled after wetting. However, high-carbon steel blades are easier to sharpen.

- **Fit:**

  Handles should be easy to grasp and, in the case of spades, shovels, and forks, long enough for you to use them without stooping but not so long that the tool is unwieldy.

- **Price:**

  Buy the best you can afford. A really fine tool is not only easier to use, it will last a lifetime if cared for properly, making that initial investment a real bargain.

Toolshed Basics

A good tool makes every gardening task easier; a bad one turns a simple task into a major chore. For example, a sturdy spade fitted to the user bites into the soil with ease, so that digging a bed is a pleasure. A flimsy spade, or one with a handle that's too long or too short, makes digging a form of punishment; by day's end, you can think only of the chiropractor. The distinction is obvious, and it shows why the way you equip your toolshed is so important to gardening. The tools you choose will shape your experience and the quality of your garden for years to come.

The common pattern is to acquire tools ad hoc. Saturday morning rolls around and the yard is covered with fallen leaves, so you run to the hardware store and grab whatever rake you find. You may get a functional tool, though the sad fact is that the average mass-marketed gardening tool is badly designed and badly manufactured. One thing is certain: Buying on impulse will fill the toolshed with a mismatched menagerie of stopgaps. You will be working not with what you need but with whatever you can find. However, if you spend a bit of time educating yourself about tools and planning your purchases, you'll not only get the best-quality tools, and tools that fit you, you'll also have just what you need right at hand when you need it. Your tools will work together as a team.

Top Tools for New Gardeners

Long-handled shovel

Leaf rake

Bypass pruner

Trowel

Cultivator

Tool Glossary

1. **Garden Fork:** More efficient than a spade at turning soil and breaking up clods; easier to force into dense soil. Look for a D-shaped handle, and for tines that are square in cross-section—flat tines bend when they strike a rock or a root. Fork should attach to handle with a closed socket or double straps, one above the handle, another below, with rivets running through it.

2. **Spade:** The tool you'll use for most digging. Blade should be thick steel, almost flat, with a straight, sharp cutting edge. There should be generous treads at the top of the blade, where you step to push it into the soil, and the blade should attach to the handle with a closed socket and long straps that run up the bottom and top of the handle to reinforce the joint. The handle should split at the top to end in an easy-to-grip D.

3. **Biodegradable Twine:** Natural fibers such as jute or cotton are softer and less likely to cut plant stems than are synthetics like nylon. Natural-fiber twines can also be composted with dead stems and prunings.

4. **Long-Handled Shovel:** Good for breaking into hard soil or for shifting piles of soil, sand, or compost. The blade should be made of a single forged and tempered piece of steel, and the socket should be closed at the back. Fiberglass handles are less likely to break when you are prying out a rock.

5. **Garden Rake:** A necessity for combing rocks and clods out of a bed and leveling the soil for seed sowing. A "bowheaded" rake is sturdier and more stable, making it better for difficult or stony soils.

6. **Trowel:** The essential planting tool. A trowel whose blade attaches with a forged socket is far stronger than cheap trowels whose stamped steel blades attach with a spikelike "tang." Cast-aluminum trowels are a lightweight but durable alternative.

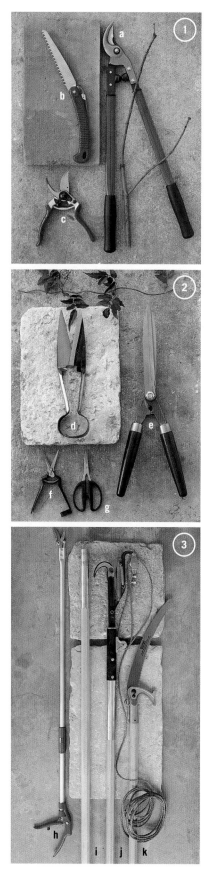

① Hand-Pruning Tools

(a) Lopper: Long-handled shears for cutting branches that are too thick for pruning shears. Lopper handles range in length from 16 to 36 inches; the longer-handled loppers are more powerful but can be heavy. Get a model with lightweight aluminum or carbon-composite handles. **(b) Pruning Saw:** Necessary for cutting branches 2 inches thick or thicker. A 12- or 13-inch blade is the most useful, as longer saws won't fit into tight corners. Saws with "Japanese," or tri-edge, blades are sharpened on three bevels instead of just one and make a fine, fast, narrow cut. Because they cut on both the push and pull, they are more efficient, too. **(c) Pruning Shears:** For cutting branches up to ¹/₂ inch thick. "Bypass" shears, which cut like scissors, make cleaner cuts and don't crush stems, allowing plants to heal more quickly. For longer service, get a model with a replaceable blade. "Anvil" pruners, which cut by pressing the branch between a blade and a broad, flat anvil, are typically cheaper but cut less cleanly.

② Hand Shears

(d) Sheep Shears: Large scissors formed from a single piece of forged, springy steel. Unbeatable for trimming grass along an edge. **(e) Hedge Shears:** Electric or gas-powered shears are faster but don't give as neat a cut. Carbon-composite handles make for lighter shears that are less tiring to use; rubber stoppers between the handles to cushion the impact on closing and protect your knuckles. **(f and g) Floral Shears:** Indispensable in the cutting garden.

③ Pole Pruners

(h, j, k) Long-Reach Pruner, Pole Pruner, and Pole Saw: These increase your reach without the danger of climbing. However, poles longer than 16 feet are flimsy and awkward to use. Wooden poles are safer than aluminum; the wood doesn't conduct electricity if you touch a power line. **(i) Extension Rod:** Attaches to pole pruner or saw.

④ Hand Tools

(l) Bulb Planter: Bores a cylindrical hole for one bulb; side markings indicate depth. **(m) Dibber:** Pointed end makes a small planting hole for seeds, seedlings, or small bulbs. **(n) Weeding Trowel:** Narrow blade slips between plants in beds. **(o) Trowel:** See page 36. **(p and q) Cultivators:** Curved claws scratch up crusted soil and uproot young weeds in a densely planted bed. **(r) Cast-Aluminum Trowel:** Lightweight; ergonomically designed for easy handling.

⑤ Ground-Surface Tools

(s) Hoe: A long-handled hoe with a pointed blade is good for precision weeding or opening a furrow for seed planting. The "stirrup" or "oscillating" hoe that slices back and forth just below the soil surface is the most efficient tool for weeding large areas. **(t) Leaf Rake:** Metal-tined rakes are the best for heavy work; bamboo rakes are lighter and less tiring to wield. Flexible tines are a must, since they pick up and move debris easily without damaging turf. **(u) Edging Spade:** A half-moon-shaped stamped steel blade set with a socket onto a long wooden handle. Essential for cutting a clean even edge to the turf around the perimeter of a bed or path.

Other Tools:

- Pocketknife: Forget the bulky, easy-to-break Swiss Army knife; get a florist's knife with a single, razor-sharp, straight-edged blade.
- Japanese Weeder: Simultaneously extracts weeds from tight spots, such as the area around the base of a plant, and cultivates the soil surface.
- Japanese Weeding Knife: Also known as a hori hori. The 6-inch-long steel blade is serrated on one side and beveled on the other. Perfect for digging deep-rooted weeds and dividing tough perennials.

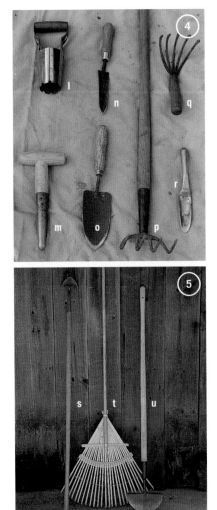

about two-thirds of a quart of motor oil—enough to just dampen the sand. Whenever you finish with a digging tool, scrape the mud off it with a plastic joint knife (sold for pennies at any building-supply center). Then plunge the tool's blade, teeth, or tines into the sand a few times. By lightly scrubbing and oiling in this fashion, you protect metal parts from rust and corrosion. Brush off the sand, and the tool is ready to hang up.

• Solvents such as lighter fluid are good for cleaning sap and pitch off the blades of pruning tools. To remove rust from neglected tools, dampen a steel-wool scouring pad with lighter fluid, and scrub. Lighter fluid also helps ease frozen or sticky joints.

Keep them sharp

• Light touch-ups of knife or shear blades are quickly done with a handheld diamond hone. To restore a badly dulled or nicked edge, you may have to use an electric bench grinder. Or clamp the blade in a vise, and sharpen it with an electric drill equipped with a 24-grit aluminum-oxide sanding disk. Either way, follow the blade's original bevel, the angle to which the manufacturer ground the edge, and remove only as much metal as necessary.

• Sharpen spades and hoes with a flat, 8- to 10-inch bastard file (its teeth are fairly coarse). Keep the file tilted at the same angle as the tool's beveled edge as you work. Grind the edge with long, sweeping strokes, applying pressure only as you push the file forward across the edge. Use the same file for shovels and edging spades, but sharpen their blades on both the front and back faces.

Fix cracked handles promptly

• Replace severely cracked handles immediately, before a break occurs and a metal blade or head flies off and injures someone.

• Wrap minor cracks with hockey-stick tape, available at sporting-goods stores. Begin several inches beyond the crack; tightly wrap the tape around the handle, with each revolution overlapping; repeat with a second layer of tape.

Caring for Tools

Once you've found a tool that suits you, you'll want to keep it. And with care, a good spade or fork or knife can last a lifetime, or even longer. Martha still uses a number of hand tools she inherited from her father.

The key to such longevity is regular maintenance. It's not hard. A few minutes' attention at the end of a day's gardening is all it takes to keep equipment looking and working like new. Well-maintained tools not only last much longer, they are easier to use.

Clean tools after use

• Fill a 5-gallon bucket with sand, and place it near the entrance to your toolshed. Mix in

Planting Primer

The next time you survey your garden, remember: The most important part is out of sight. Leaves, stems, and flowers all play essential roles in the life cycle of a plant, but none can function without the water, nutrients, and support provided by roots. That's why planting well, giving the roots of your plants a good grip on the soil, deserves special attention.

You begin, of course, by preparing the soil (as explained at the beginning of this chapter). Depending on what you are planting, however, soil preparation takes different forms. If you are planting annual and perennial flowers, or a formal display of roses, you prepare a bed. That is, you create an expanse of thoroughly improved soil that provides the loose, airy texture, enhanced fertility, and excellent drainage such high-performance plantings require. A bed provides plenty of root-room for these smaller plants.

Larger landscape specimens, however, including most shrubs and trees, need to spread their roots across a broader area than a bed can provide. You must integrate these plants into the site's natural soil. To accomplish this, you select species adapted to the local soil type, and then take care not to alter too much the soil within the planting hole. If the soil is compacted or poor, you may add organic matter in the form of compost or sphagnum peat, but make sure that the dose amounts to no more than 25 percent of the whole. Your goal is to avoid creating a marked distinction between the soil inside the hole and the soil outside it, because so abrupt a change can act as a barrier, stopping the roots from spreading out into the surrounding area.

Traditionally, the soil in a bed was turned to a depth of 2 feet or more. But over the past generation, research has shown that most plant roots stay within 6 to 12 inches of the surface. For this reason, it's now believed that turning a bed to a depth of about 1 foot is ample. Likewise, the old rule that trees and shrubs should be planted in deep pits has been discarded. Modern planting holes are saucer-shaped, three times as wide as the plant's root ball but just deep enough to accommodate the roots. When the root ball is resting on the bottom of the hole, the top of the ball should be level with the surrounding soil surface.

Most nurseries grow their plants in plastic containers today, though trees and shrubs are also often sold "B&B"; that is, balled and burlapped. Mail-order roses and perennials may arrive "bare-root"—dug up while dormant and shipped without soil around the roots. Each of these variations requires slightly different treatment at planting time.

Container-grown plants are the most convenient. Transferring them from pot to soil causes relatively little trauma to their roots, so that container-grown specimens may be planted at virtually any time throughout the growing season. Digging and wrapping causes extensive damage to the roots of B&B plants, so they should be replanted promptly, at a time when the weather won't stress the plants, as during the cool, moist seasons of spring or early fall.

Timing is even more important with bare-root plants. Their roots must be back in the soil before the plants awaken from dormancy, and generally,

Opposite: Martha arranges seedlings before planting them at Turkey Hill. Left: Rake the soil in a bed to remove stones before planting annuals or perennials. Any time you plant is a perfect moment to improve the fertility of the garden soil by adding compost, well-aged manure, or other organic amendments. Of course, you are also giving the new transplant a boost. When you work the planting area as you dig, you "open" the soil's texture, helping water and nutrients penetrate to the roots and encouraging them to spread.

Maintenance

It's not the most glamorous part of gardening, but maintenance is essential. Plants respond far better to moderate but consistent care than they do to occasional bouts of heroic intervention. Suddenly saturating the vegetable garden with a flood of water after you've allowed the soil to get bone-dry does your crops as much harm as good. But turn on the soaker hoses to moisten the soil deeply as the leaves start to flag, give the garden the inch of water it needs during every week of rainless weather, and not only will you reap bigger harvests, but the fruits and vegetables you pick will actually taste better.

Weeding is definitely an activity in which it is far easier to keep up than catch up. Attack the weeds with your hoe or cultivator just as they pop out of the ground, when their roots are still shallow, and you can scratch out a bed's worth in a few minutes. Let weeds go, though, and you'll be digging and pulling, and still leaving behind fragments of tenacious roots that will certainly resprout. What's more, during the time you let the weeds flourish, they will stunt the flowers that are their neighbors, robbing them of valuable water, nutrients, and light. Neglected weeds also serve as a hideout for

such plants are sold only in the early spring. As soon as bare-root plants arrive from the nursery, open the shipping carton, and inspect its contents. The roots should be smooth and greenish; if they are shriveled and black, call the nursery and ask for replacements. If you can't plant for a few days, moisten the roots with a mist of water, repack the plants in the shipping carton, and store it in a dry, cool spot. It's best, though, to plant bare-root nursery stock right away.

Many gardeners favor giving new plantings a boost by soaking the soil around them with a balanced, water-soluble fertilizer mixed at half the strength recommended on the product label. An even more important kind of after-planting care, however, is regular watering. Give new plantings at least an inch of water per week during dry weather. If you get an inch of rain per week, then irrigation is unnecessary.

An easy way to increase water flow to the roots of a new tree or shrub is to mound up the soil around the planting hole into a low, circular dike. This traps rainfall and irrigation water, holding it until it soaks in rather than just running off. For the best results, position this dike right over the perimeter of the plant's root ball. Most nurseries grow trees and shrubs in soil mixes heavily amended with peat. Such mixes dry out faster than ordinary soils and don't absorb moisture as easily from their surroundings. Positioning your dike correctly ensures that your new planting won't suffer from this sort of man-made drought.

pests and diseases that sally forth to attack the rest of the garden.

The best way to handle maintenance is to make it a routine, so that you anticipate needs. Fertilization, for example, is most effective if you feed plants at the beginning of their seasons of active growth, such as spring. Don't wait for the foliage to yellow or for other signs of malnutrition to appear before you come to the rescue, as by then the plants will already have been traumatized.

Many such tasks can be scheduled well in advance, for they must be done every year at about the same time. But the day-to-day life of a garden is unpredictable—no one can foresee what the weather and wildlife will do, and every plant has its own personality. Just like children, they will eventually make it known that attention must be paid. So devote a few minutes each weekend for a tour of inspection in the garden to look for insect infestations, thirsty plants, weed colonies, and other pressing needs as they develop.

The daily rounds you make in the garden can head off weeks of labor-intensive weeding, watering, and pruning. And you will be pleasantly surprised by the results. What others will call your green thumb is mainly a matter of paying attention.

planting bulbs

The timing couldn't be simpler: Plant spring-flowering bulbs, such as hyacinths and tulips, in the fall; and summer-flowering bulbs, such as gladioli and dahlias, in the spring. But don't waste a minute planting inferior-quality bulbs, which may disappoint you with a poor performance—or no performance at all. The best bulbs are firm and plump. Select the right tool for planting, too. Small, or "minor," bulbs such as snowdrops and winter aconite are easily slipped into a shallow crevice in the soil made with the tip of a trowel. Larger bulbs, like many alliums, need to be sunk deeper, in holes bored with a bulb planter or dug with a shovel.

1 Select bulbs, and bag them yourself at a garden center, or order them from a grower, who will box and ship them. Plant your purchase as soon as possible, since bulbs can wither when left out on a shelf or grow moldy when kept in an airtight container. If you must delay planting, store the bulbs away from the light in a cool, sheltered place, such as a garage or basement.

2 To work out a planting scheme before digging, lay the bulbs on top of the ground where they will grow. Rearrange the bulbs until you are happy with the result. Irregular, curvilinear patterns tend to create the most natural-looking drifts of flowers. Dig each planting hole to a depth that measures roughly three times the diameter of the bulb it will hold; the hole need only be wide enough for you to insert the bulb so that it touches the bottom.

3 Before placing a bulb in a hole, check which side is up. Most bulbs have a tapered tip, which should point upward; that is where foliage and flowers will later emerge (roots will grow from the opposite, flat or indented "bottom"). Backfill soil into the hole, and firm it to eliminate air pockets, and secure bulbs in their upright position. A final light dusting of bonemeal on top of the soil-filled hole will gradually supply phosphorus as it seeps down to the bulb, stimulating root growth and boosting bloom.

planting container-grown annuals and perennials

You have finished the necessary, if unromantic, groundwork for a new bed or border and you're itching for the satisfaction of putting in plants and watching them develop and flower. The quickest way to get there is to plant container-grown annuals and perennials purchased at a local nursery or garden center. Once you've brought the plants home, it's tempting to hurriedly dig holes and plop in the new arrivals. Control your eagerness, though, and take the time to perform this task carefully. Any plant is likeliest to achieve its potential if you give it a hole of the right size, and water it thoroughly.

1 Dig a hole that is at least a couple of inches wider than the container in which the plant has been grown. The hole should be just deep enough so that the top of the potting-mix-covered root mass will be level with the surface of the surrounding garden soil.

2 Because container-grown plants have been confined to pots, they tend to become root-bound. To stimulate new roots to emerge and grow outward into the garden soil, gently tease them apart with your fingertips. Tough, fibrous roots require more radical surgery: Use one blade of sharp pruning shears to slice through the dense root mass.

3 Backfill soil around the roots, firm the soil to eliminate any air pockets, and water it well, adding a balanced water-soluble fertilizer if you wish. For larger plants (purchased in one-gallon containers), create a shallow moat around the plant by mounding a ring of soil at least 2 or 3 inches high. This will conserve precious runoff whenever you water the plant and act as a catch basin for rainfall.

planting a bare-root perennial or rose

1 Mound a small cone of soil in the center of the planting hole to support the roots and ensure that every fiber touches soil. (Before planting, all bare-root roses and many thick-rooted perennials, such as Japanese iris, benefit from being submerged in a bucket of water for several hours. Keep the bucketful of water for step 3.) Splay the roots over the cone like the tentacles of an octopus.

2 While holding the plant upright, backfill the hole with soil. As you fill, use a length of bamboo to firm soil around and between the roots, taking care not to damage or break any fibers. This will help to eliminate air pockets. Be certain to keep the crown of the plant flush with the level of surrounding garden soil.

3 Make a water "well" or moat around the base of the plant by mounding a ring of soil 3 to 4 inches high. Gradually pour half of the water left over from step 1 all around the well. Let this seep into the soil, and repeat. A garden hose or watering can may also be used, so long as the irrigation is gentle and slow.

planting a balled-and-burlapped tree or shrub

1 Use a shovel handle to measure the diameter and depth of the root ball. Dig a hole slightly wider than the diameter and deep enough so that the point where the trunk emerges from the root ball will lie flush with the soil level. After placing the plant in the hole, cut the cords binding the root ball, and peel back the burlap from around its top. Roll the burlap covering down so that it will be entirely buried when the hole has been refilled.

2 Backfill with soil dug for the hole. If the soil is very heavy or very sandy, mix it with compost (no more than $1/4$ the total amount of soil). Use your heel to firm the soil around the entire circumference of the plant. Large, top-heavy plants such as trees and shrubs need a solid footing to prevent them from being blown over in high winds.

3 Mound up loose soil to form a 4- to 5-inch-high dike over the perimeter of the buried root ball. Using a hose with a water-breaker attachment adjusted for a gentle spray, gradually flood this area with water, and allow it to drain slowly into the soil. Refill.

Irrigation When you are pruning a large limb off a tree, your garden may seem all too solid, but in fact, the plant part of it at least is mostly water. Even a solid-seeming Douglas fir is really 85 percent water, while a perennial flower is nearly all water—95 percent—with just enough solid matter wrapped around it to give it shape. This makes the hose your most powerful gardening tool. For how you irrigate—how much water you give your garden and how you apply it—does more to determine the look of the garden than anything else.

Stint on the water, and you will stunt your plants, but give them more than they need and you'll encourage overly lush, soft growth that is easy prey for diseases, deer, insects, and other pests. The object is to give plants what they need, when they need it, and no more. That may sound dauntingly precise, but in fact, success as an irrigator is largely just a matter of matching the right technology to each situation and each variety of plant.

Drip Irrigation

Installing one of these networks of tubing and tiny nozzles ("emitters") takes some planning and some work, but it allows pinpoint precision in water application. Originally developed to conserve water, drip irrigation, as the name suggests, drips water directly onto the soil above the plant roots, at a rate slow enough (if the system has been designed correctly) that none is lost as runoff. Drip irrigation reduces a garden's water use by as much as two-thirds, which makes it a necessity throughout much of the Southwest and other regions where water is scarce.

A common problem with drip irrigation is that individual emitters may clog, leaving a gap in your irrigation. To prevent this, use self-cleaning emitters, which clear themselves every time the system is turned on. On sloping sites, "pressure-compensating" emitters are also a must, as otherwise gravity will increase the flow from emitters downhill, destroying the precision of your water application.

Avoid the temptation to place emitters right at the bases of the plants, as that keeps the plants too wet, fostering a fungal disease known as crown rot. In addition, setting emitters right by the plants discourages them from extending their roots out through the surrounding soil, which makes the plants less able to forage for nutrients. Even

Snaking along a border, drip-line irrigation gradually emits water right at the soil surface. As water seeps into the soil, it gives roots a steady supply of moisture while minimizing the wasteful evaporation and runoff that can result from overhead watering.

automatic watering

Anatomy of a Drip System

(a) The Controls: A well-designed automated drip-irrigation system has controls built into a single unit. Key components include a water-flow regulator, a timer, a filter, and an anti-backflow device, which prevents water from being siphoned from the system.

(b) Emitters: Spaced at regular intervals, emitters are held inside plastic tubing. Metal pins that fit over the tubes are pushed into the soil to secure them.

Mulch keeps the system out of sight.

(c) Extensions: Smaller emitters can run from the main line to irrigate pots, window boxes, or other containers. Because the water-flow regulator can be set to deliver different rates of irrigation to separate zones, it is possible to suit the different requirements of containers and beds simultaneously.

(d) Connections: A T-shaped joint connects the plastic emitter tubes to the rigid PVC pipes that feed them.

(e) The Working System: A fully automated drip-line irrigation system is simplest to lay out and install when the garden plan is rectangular.

(f) The Plan: In this basic yet efficient layout, lines run between evenly spaced planting rows. An automatic timer schedules regular watering, even while the gardener is away. Plastic tubing must be drained before the onset of winter's chill, to prevent cracking and ruptures.

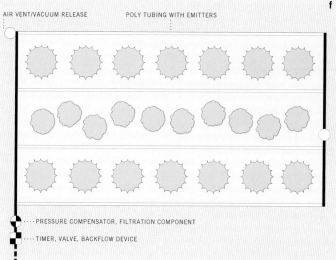

AIR VENT/VACUUM RELEASE   POLY TUBING WITH EMITTERS

···· PRESSURE COMPENSATOR, FILTRATION COMPONENT

···· TIMER, VALVE, BACKFLOW DEVICE

fertilizers don't help plants irrigated in this fashion unless they are delivered with the water through the emitters. Instead, deploy a system of "in-line" emitters, in which the emitters have been integrated right into the irrigation tubes, and cover the area to be watered with a regular pattern of parallel watering lines. Spaced 12, 18, or 24 inches apart, the lines are stretched across a bed. In sandy soil, where water tends to drain straight downward, use tubing that includes emitters every 12 inches, and space the tubes 12 to 14 inches apart. With denser soils such as clays, where water tends to move laterally, use tubing with emitters set at 18-inch intervals, and space the tubes 18 to 24 inches apart. Run the tubes down $1/2$-inch-deep grooves scratched into the soil surface, and cover them with an organic mulch; nobody else will know they are there.

In-Ground Sprinkler Systems

When professionally designed and installed, such systems offer conservation as well as convenience. The pattern of water distribution is tailored to the shape of your yard, and the amount of water each area gets can be precisely adjusted. As a result, a good in-ground system generally uses 20 to 50 percent less water to irrigate a garden than would portable sprinklers.

Timers

Electronic timers, which turn a drip system or in-ground sprinkler system on and off at preset intervals, offer convenience and ensure that the garden is watered while you are away. Better models can deliver different amounts of water to different areas of the garden and include a rain switch, a device that prevents the system from turning on during or just after a rainstorm. Switch the timer to the manual mode when you are at home, though, so that you decide when and how much to irrigate. The timer cannot distinguish between a bright, breezy, dry day (when your plants are especially thirsty) and a gray, cool, humid one (when your plants' need for water is far less). After all, you shouldn't turn your most powerful gardening tool over to a microchip.

Portable Sprinklers

Conventional portable sprinklers are inefficient. They irrigate by flinging water droplets through the air, and on a hot, breezy day, half the droplets may evaporate before they even reach the ground. Many of the remaining droplets are likely to run off across the surface, since sprinklers commonly discharge water faster than a garden's soil can absorb it. This makes them a poor alternative for regions where water is in short supply. Sprinklers are great for spot watering, though: When you find a patch of thirsty plants, you can set a sprinkler there, and administer water just to those in need. For this reason, portable sprinklers remain a useful backup for drip systems.

For large expanses of lawn or ground cover, impulse sprinklers are the most effective. When firmly mounted on a "tower"—a tripod up to six feet tall—an impulse sprinkler can wet the area out to a radius of 80 feet or more. Because the stream of droplets is fired out at a lower trajectory, impulse sprinklers are also the best for a windy day; the droplets are less likely to be blown off course.

Oscillating sprinklers, whose curved arm rocks back and forth to spread water in a waving fan, don't cope well with wind because of their high trajectory. But the better models can be set to water a long, narrow strip or one side only. On a still day, these are the best sprinklers for watering a flower border or a bed of shrubbery.

Sprinkler Glossary

① Hoses and Attachments

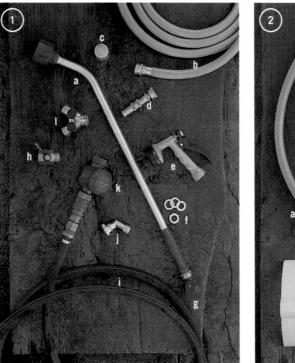

(a) Water Wand: Provides 24 to 48 inches of extended reach. Soft stream perfect for containers and newly planted trees, shrubs, and flowers. **(b) Garden Hose:** Best quality has 3- to 5-ply reinforced interior, vinyl coating, and corrosion-resistant brass fittings. Standard lengths: 25, 50, and 100 feet. **(c) Water Breaker:** Attached to end of hose, moderates forceful stream into a gentler flow. **(d) Nozzle:** Rotating brass barrels provide a range of watering patterns, from full stream to mist. **(e) Spray Trigger:** Squeeze-control adjusts nozzle; lock clip allows continuous flow. **(f) Washer:** Rubber ring; prevents leaks at hose and sprinkler connections. **(g) Plastic Shutoff Valve:** Lightweight, durable; regulates flow from fully open to completely closed. **(h) Shutoff Valve:** Heavy-duty brass. **(i) Soaker Hose:** Porous casing provides even watering directly into soil; soaks area up to 4 feet from hose. **(j) Gooseneck Adapter:** Swiveling neck keeps hose from kinking at spigot. **(k) Timer:** Turns water on or off automatically. **(l) "Y" Connector:** Allows two hoses to tap one source; built-in shutoff valves; corrosion-resistant zinc.

② Sprinklers

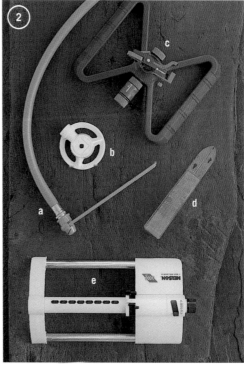

(a) Norwood Sprinkler Head: Attaches to end of garden hose; spike inserted into soil holds sprinkler in place. **(b) Square-Spray Sprinkler:** Radial spray works well in corners or small gardens. **(c) Impulse Sprinkler:** Evenly waters areas up to 80 inches in diameter; quick-connect fitting for hose hookup. **(d) Rain Gauge:** Measures precipitation and irrigation; spiked end can be inserted into soil or mounted on a post. **(e) Oscillating Sprinkler:** Adjusts for coverage from 75 to 3,600 square feet; 20 precision jets can be narrowed or widened to adapt spray.

③ Watering Cans and Sprayers

(a) Pump Sprayer: Trigger activated; nozzle adjusts for mist or spray jet; ideal for moistening soil surface and misting seedlings. **(b) Plastic Watering Can:** 2-quart capacity; rust- and dent-proof; lighter than metal. Long spout with brass rose (sprinkler attachment) ideal for outdoor container watering. **(c) Galvanized-Metal Watering Can:** 2½-gallon capacity; handle design allows for one-handed use. **(d) Copper Watering Can:** 3-pint capacity; splash-proof rim; perfect for houseplants. **(e) Spray Bottle:** Useful for misting community seedling pots and houseplants.

watering

Whether it's a vegetable, a flower, a shrub, or a tree—and whether it grows in a container or in the ground—every plant needs water. Seed germination, flower and fruit development, and seed production all depend on a steady supply of moisture. But water can also be harmful if it is administered improperly. For example, a harsh jet of water from a hose aimed at the top of a root ball can rapidly wash away soil, exposing the roots to drying, damaging sun and wind. On the other hand, roots standing in waterlogged soil are likely to rot and, eventually, kill the plant.

Watering can: Always attach a rose, or breaker, the perforated end piece that fits onto the spout. Water is "broken" into droplets as it passes through the tiny holes, creating a gentle stream that avoids exposing roots and lets soil absorb moisture evenly.

Bottom watering: This is especially effective for young seedlings in cell packs as well as mature houseplants. Place the cell pack or pot in a deep, watertight tray, bin, or basin. Slowly pour water from a watering can until the water is halfway up the side of the large container. Allow the water to be absorbed until the soil's surface is slightly moist to the touch (do not let plants sit in water overnight). Promptly remove the cell pack or pot from the water, allowing excess to drain off.

Water well: Make a moat to help a newly planted perennial, shrub, or tree get established, while minimizing runoff. After planting, hill up a ring of soil around the base of the plant about as wide as the root mass. The ring should be 3 to 4 inches high, depending on the plant's size. Carefully place a trickling garden hose inside the well, and gently flood it with water. Allow the water to soak in, and repeat.

Overhead watering: This makes most sense where large areas make soil-level irrigation impractical. It is best to water early in the morning, allowing the sun and wind to dry off plant foliage throughout the day (dry foliage is less prone to diseases and harmful fungi). Saturate the soil; deep watering promotes strong roots.

Health Tips

You take vitamins and exercise to keep yourself healthy. Your plants need a similar regimen. Observing a few simple guidelines will help to keep your garden luxuriant—and spare you the dreary, time-consuming task of tending to the sick.

Plant at the recommended spacing. To find room for extra treasures, it's tempting to pack in plants closer than the nursery labels recommend. Don't! Crowding the roots reduces their ability to find the nutrients and moisture the plant needs, and that is likely to stunt the plant and reduce or abort entirely its crop of flowers and fruits.

Allow for air circulation. An easy flow of air around a plant provides natural protection against disease by keeping its foliage dry; continuous moisture provides a perfect breeding ground for fungal and bacterial pathogens. Good air circulation also enhances disease resistance by blowing away fungal spores. Improve air circulation by using permeable barriers such as hedges or louvered fencing for enclosure. Make sure to keep space for air circulation between disease-prone plants, such as roses.

Don't wet the foliage when you water. This also promotes diseases. Water disease-prone plants with a soaker hose or a drip-irrigation system.

Provide for good drainage. Soil that remains persistently wet encourages root and crown rot in all except wetland plants, and cold penetrates into such soil more deeply in wintertime, increasing the risk of frost damage. Good drainage is crucial to plant health; guarantee it on low-lying sites by constructing raised beds.

Keep up with sanitation. Weeds and organic debris are a haven for plant pests and disease pathogens. Especially harmful is debris from infected plants, which if left in place will serve as a source of reinfection year after year. Black spot-infected rose leaves, for example, become a reservoir of black-spot spores. Bag such debris, and dispose of it or burn it.

Attract insect predators. The easiest way to control insect pests is to attract other insects that prey on the pests. As much as possible, avoid toxic sprays and dusts that kill predators and pests alike. Plant species rich in pollen and nectar, such as catnip, dill, and yarrow, are used by many predaceous insects as an alternate food source at certain stages in their lives. Set out a large bowl of pebbles, and fill it with water until only the tops of the pebbles are exposed so that the insects will have a place to light and drink without drowning. Finally, get a field guide to insects and a hand lens. The insect you suspect of attacking your plants may be friend instead of foe.

Deadheading

For plants, flowering is strictly business. They bloom to attract the pollinators that help them bear fertile seeds. To prevent this consummation by deadheading—the removal of spent or fading flowers and with them the immature seedheads they enclose—may seem unkind. In fact, though, deadheading is as crucial to the beauty of your garden as it is to the vigor of the plants.

With plants that bloom repeatedly through the growing season, for example, a category that includes most annual flowers and most nearly all modern roses, deadheading promotes more continuous bloom. Typically, seed production causes a sort of botanical menopause that ends or severely reduces flower production for the remainder of that growing season. In many annuals, the production of seed signals the completion of the plant's life cycle, and the annual actually dies soon thereafter.

Many perennials such as daylilies and irises and all the spring bulbs are "determinate" plants, meaning that they bloom for a set or determinate period each season. Deadheading won't prolong their flowering, but it will prevent the plants from depleting their stored energy to produce seeds that you do not want. This energy conservation greatly improves the plant's chance of surviving the winter and also enhances the quality of the next year's floral display.

When planting vegetable seedlings, such as these lettuces, use your thumb and little finger to measure the spacing between plants. This interval allows the right amounts of sunlight, water, and air to reach the soil as well as the plants as they grow.

Snapping seed pods: Many de-terminate perennials such as daylilies and bearded and Siberian irises end their period of bloom by producing prominent seed pods. As soon as the petals fall, use your thumb and forefinger to snap each pod off the flower stem. Because the various flowers on a stem open sequentially, this deadhead-ing may continue over a period of days or weeks. When you've removed all the flowers on a stem, use a bypass pruner to cut the stem near its base.

Pinching annuals: To dead-head most annuals, catch the stem between the edge of your thumbnail and the tip of your fore-finger, and gently apply pressure until you've nipped off the spent flower. The goal is a clean sep-aration—torn or ragged edges can encourage disease.

Deadheading spring bulbs: When a flower's color fades and its petals droop, snip it off with a sharp pair of floral shears (for stems thicker than 1/4 inch, use bypass pruners). Cut 1 inch below the flower's base. Not all bulbs require deadheading, however: The smaller ones, such as crocus, scilla, and *Narcissus bulbocodi-um,* will reflower successfully even when left to their own devices.

Deadheading roses: For once-blooming roses, the wild-type species roses, and old garden ros-es such as gallicas that bloom just once each growing season, removing spent flowers is a matter of neatness. For reblooming mod-ern roses such as floribundas and hybrid teas, it's crucial to pro-longing their display. With bypass pruners, cut back to a point on the stem just above a leaf with five leaflets—this promotes strong re-growth and helps ensure that the next flower will be of good size. A note for northern gardeners: Stop deadheading in late summer, as setting seed encourages the bush to go dormant and enhances its cold tolerance.

Shearing: This drastic form of deadheading can force a second bloom from some indeterminate perennials, such as *Coreopsis ver-ticillata* 'Moonbeam,' and some shrubs, such as potentilla. A midsummer shearing can also revive bedraggled annuals. To shear, gather handfuls of stems, and slice them cleanly. Follow the plant's natural contours, whether spreading or mounding, and shape as you go. Avoid taking off more than two-thirds of the stems.

Cutting tough-stemmed annuals: Use sharp bypass pruning shears to sever the sturdy stems of annuals like zinnias and sunflowers that resist normal pinching. Cut about 1/8 inch above a leaf, to promote new growth and flowering.

Fertilizing

With all the products for sale at the average garden center, selecting the fertilizer for your garden can be bewildering. But forget the advertising—what you need to understand is plant nutrition.

Given sufficient light and raw materials, plants actually make their own sugars, proteins, and carbohydrates. To do this, they need six key elements: carbon, hydrogen, oxygen, nitrogen, phosphorous, and potassium. Plants take carbon, hydrogen, and oxygen from the air and from water. They take nitrogen, phosphorus, and potassium, known as macronutrients, from the soil; these are what must be replenished with fertilizer. The macronutrients' chemical symbols—N, P, and K—are on every fertilizer label, along with a set of three numbers—10–6–4, 10–10–10, 5–10–10, etc.—which indicate the percentage (by weight) that product contains of each. So-called "complete" fertilizers supply all three macronutrients; incomplete fertilizers provide only one or two macronutrients and must be combined with other products if you are to satisfy all your plants' needs.

Plants also require other nutrients in lesser quantities. Calcium, magnesium, and sulfur may need to be added to soil, along with even smaller amounts of seven micronutrients—boron, chlorine, copper, iron, manganese, molybdenum, and zinc.

Plants use the various nutrients in different ways. Nitrogen promotes the growth of green leaves and stems, so leafy vegetables take in a lot. Phosphorus promotes early root growth and helps plants set buds and blooms, making it essential for healthy fruit and flowers. Potassium aids in overall vigor; it helps plants make carbohydrates, provides some disease resistance, and encourages healthy roots. The micronutrients satisfy a wide variety of needs; unless a soil test shows a specific deficit, all the micronutrients your plants require can be supplied by working compost or other organic matter into the soil before planting.

An important distinction among fertilizers lies in the source of their nutrients. "Organic" fertilizers derive their ingredients from plants, animals, and animal by-products; they include feather meal, bonemeal, and blood meal. "Natural" is commonly used to describe rock powders (see page 25). Synthetic fertilizers contain man-made ingredients, like urea (a common nitrogen source). To determine the sources of a fertilizer's nutrients, check the "Derived from" section of the label.

Besides supplying plant nutrients, organic and natural fertilizers improve the quality of the soil. And since these fertilizers must be broken down by microorganisms in the soil before plants can absorb their nutrients, they release their nutrients slowly, with almost no risk of overfertilizing. By feeding the microorganisms they add vitality to the soil, and as they decay the organics build humus. However, organic and natural fertilizers contain lower percentages of nutrients than do the synthetics; typically, the three numbers of an organic's formula total less than fifteen. You must apply more of the organics when you fertilize even though, because of the slower nutrient release, you apply them less frequently.

Synthetic fertilizers usually have more nutrients per pound and their nutrients are water soluble, a form that the plants can use right away. This makes them ideal for giving needy plants a quick boost. Indeed, water-soluble nitrogen is so easily absorbed by plants that in excess it will injure roots. Furthermore, if not absorbed by plants, water-soluble nutrients soon wash out of the soil and can then pollute surface and groundwater. Never apply more than the recommended amount of a synthetic fertilizer. Also, when choosing a synthetic, check the "Guaranteed Analysis" on the label to see how much of the nitrogen is water insoluble or slow release, and select a product that favors those forms.

Synthetics are definitely superior for plants such as lettuce that need early spring feedings. The cold soil of that season inhibits microbial action and so prevents the breakdown of natural and organic fertilizers. By contrast, the lower soil temperature has no effect on the availability of synthetics' nutrients.

Weeding Strategies

Despite all the potent (too potent) herbicides on the market, the most efficient and effective strategy for dealing with weeds remains prevention. Keep those unwanted plants from getting established in your garden, and you won't need poisons. You'll have to do some cleanup, some pulling and hoeing, because weeds are persistent, and no system of exclusion is perfect. But the problem will be minor, and you won't have to resort to chemical warfare.

Start with a clean slate. Whenever you create a new bed, bringing it into cultivation, first eliminate all the weeds there by "solarizing" the soil. This should be done at midsummer. Strip away any existing plant growth from the prospective bed, and dig or till the soil. Rake the soil smooth, and water it if it is dry. Dig a trench a few inches deep around the new bed's perimeter. Then cover the whole bed with a sheet of clear plastic. Press this down so that it is in close contact with the soil and its edges are in the trench. Secure the sheet by refilling the trench. Left in place for four to eight weeks, this plastic cover will trap solar energy and slowly "cook" any weeds that have survived your tilling. Solarization also kills the countless weed seeds that are undoubtedly lying dormant in the bed's soil, so that the weeds don't rise again like Lazarus after you have planted.

Don't create opportunities for weeds. Leaving areas of soil, especially tilled soil, unplanted is an invitation to weedy invaders. Weed seeds are continually blowing and washing into your yard, even hitchhiking on animals that pass through, and they will soon find any unoccupied niches. Keep your soil fully planted—the presence of other plants discourages the germination of the new arrivals— or cover it with a layer of organic mulch, so that the weed seeds never come in contact with the earth.

Water precisely. Give your plants just the water they need, and deliver it right to the area of their roots with soaker hoses or a drip-irrigation system. Spreading a lot of unnecessary water around the landscape is like watering the weeds. Remember, without moisture, even weeds cannot grow.

Weed often, and you will devote far less time in total to this boring chore. While weeds are still small, a quick pass with a hoe down the aisles of your vegetable garden will do them in. A quick twist will uproot a weed seedling, whereas a mature weed may have to be dug out. Above all, make sure to get to weeds before they set seed. Remember the old gardener's axiom: "One year's seeding, seven years' weeding." One weed plant can produce tens of thousands of seeds, and you are going to regret every one of them.

Mulching

Experienced gardeners know that a blanket of mulch is one of the most effective ways to suppress weed growth. But that's only one reason for mulching the garden. Mulch, especially a layer of some fluffy organic matter spread at least an inch deep, insulates the soil, keeping the summer sun from heating it to a temperature that would inhibit root growth. In addition, by blocking the evaporation of water off the soil surface, mulch is a great aid to water conservation. In arid climates, mulching can reduce your garden's water needs by as much as a half. Finally, as it decomposes, an organic mulch adds humus to the soil—in effect, composting continuously all over the garden.

In addition to all the horticultural benefits it provides, mulch can also be decorative. Tucked in neatly around the plants, it's like a fresh coat of paint on a house, giving the garden a finished look. At the same time, it serves as a background that sets off individual plants while it pulls the different parts of the garden together into a whole.

mulch glossary

Shredded bark: Stripped from fallen trees and run through a shredder, the pieces generally are no longer than 1½ inches. With its natural color and tendency to knit together and stay in place, bark is both attractive and effective for holding in moisture and keeping down weeds. Great around newly planted trees and shrubs.

Salt hay: *Spartina reptens* is harvested from salt marshes along the southeastern seaboard. Unlike other, less expensive hay mulches, salt hay usually contains no seed that can sprout into weeds, making it worth the premium price. Lightweight, yet an effective insulator.

Buckwheat hulls: Light in weight, hulls are easier to haul and spread than many mulches, though they can be blown out of place by high wind (to help them stay put, moisten the hulls with water). Reapply mulch every two or three seasons. Barely pea-size, the hulls are small enough for mulching houseplants, too. Many dark-colored mulches soon turn tan or gray, but buckwheat's handsome dark brown resists fading.

Grass clippings: Leave clippings in place after mowing to feed the lawn as they decay, or collect them to mulch the vegetable garden. Fast rate of decomposition releases nitrogen quickly. To avoid excessive heat from decomposition, spread a mat no thicker than 2 to 3 inches. Excellent moisture retention.

Pine needles: Light and easy to use. Needles resist matting down in damp, winter weather; use them to backfill a protective burlap "sleeve" around a tree peony or a rose. If a pine tree grows in your yard, you'll soon have plenty of fallen needles.

Aged manure: A rich source of nitrogen, easily obtained and applied. Manure can act as both mulch and soil conditioner. Just be certain that the manure chosen is aged (or composted). Fresh cow manure will "burn" plants it comes in contact with, introduce weed seeds into the garden, and remove helpful microbes from the soil as it breaks down and decomposes.

Leaves: Probably the best mulch bargain going. To prevent matting, shred with your lawn mower or a mechanical shredder. A layer 3 to 4 inches thick, put down in fall, can insulate plantings not only from cold weather, but also from drying, damaging winter winds. In mid-spring to summer, lighter layers can be added to hold in moisture and help to exclude weeds. Keep a stockpile of composting leaves in a back corner of the yard for a year-round supply of leaf mold.

Supports

We all need someone we can lean on, and plants are no exception. The supports you provide for your plants—trellises, bamboo tripods, and other constructions of stakes and twine—are what lift vines and climbers up into the third dimension to give your garden height and depth. These are also the tools by which you direct and contain the growth of your plants, keeping long-stemmed beauties from degenerating into messy sprawls. Supports let you stretch the space in an overcrowded garden, where you may want more plants but have nowhere left to go but up. Finally, they save time and money. A plant-covered trellis creates a living backdrop or frame for the garden picture without the commitment and expense of building walls or waiting for an evergreen hedge to mature.

Generally, the means of support fall into two categories. There are decorative supports, such as a handcrafted arbor, tuteur, or trellis, that are designed to become part of the display themselves. And then there are deliberately self-effacing structures, designed to support without distracting from the beauty of the plant, like the brushwood twigs that Martha tucks in around her young chrysanthemums to keep the stems from collapsing later when they are full grown and weighted with flowers.

Besides exposing vines and other climbing or twining plants to sunlight and air, wooden supports like this pyramid-shaped tuteur show off flowers and foliage. Such vertical structures also add pleasing height and architectural massing to the garden.

With either class of support, though, the process of training the plant is essentially the same, a balance of firmness and respect. The support must be secure, and an effective restraint. Yet it must avoid the too obvious control that turns a garden into a botanical dungeon, a place where flowers are bound to the stake without regard for their natural tendencies, or "habit."

Remember that anticipation is the key. Know the form the plant wants to take, and plan the support to suit that natural pattern of growth. Then install the support early. Later, as the plants mature, the spreading leaves will hide your bindings and scaffolding, and they will enhance rather than restrict.

materials for supports

- **Bamboo stakes:** Resilient, light, and strong, as well as inexpensive and generally available. Green-dyed bamboo is particularly inconspicuous. (To support really husky plants, such as dahlias, stakes of rot-resistant wood such as cedar, 1 inch or more thick, may be necessary.)
- **Brushwood:** Branches from twiggy, supple trees, such as birch or wild cherry, can be stuck in the ground beside sprawling plants, like chrysanthemums or peas, when they are still young. As the plants grow, the brushwood supports from below. Harvest brushwood in March or early April, when rising sap has made the wood flexible.
- **Willow shoots:** Cut just before bud burst, willow has a flexibility that makes it ideal for rustic trellises.
- **Grapevines:** May be wound around tripods to furnish stability and extra points of attachment for plants. Harvest vines while dormant; soak in water for several hours before use.
- **Twine:** This should be soft so that it doesn't abrade stems of plants being tied and organic so that at season's end it may be gathered up and disposed of in the compost bin. Jute comes in two grades: a lightweight twine, for smaller plants, and a heavier one for larger plants. Jute twine and coarser sisal work well for lashing together tripods and trellises.
- **Raffia:** Made from dried palm fronds, each strip can be split into any thickness desired. Dull khaki in color, raffia is virtually invisible in the garden and is biodegradable. Soak in warm water for a few minutes to soften before use. Available at craft stores.
- **Copper wire:** Durable lashing for supports exposed to weather. Tarnishes to an unobtrusive brown.

specialized supports

Peony ring (top left): Herbaceous peonies, and many other long-stemmed perennials, form natural bouquets. A peony ring—a ring encircling a 2½-inch grid atop stakes—contains stems so they don't topple and yet allows a graceful spread. Buy the peony ring ready-made from heavy-gauge wire, or make your own from natural materials like flexible willow twigs, bamboo stakes, and twine. Set the ring over the cluster of emerging peony stems in early spring, and push the legs deep into the ground so the ring rests 6 inches above the soil. As stems push up through the grid, pull the ring upward; it should always stand about three-quarters as tall as the plant itself.

Tuteur (center): From the French *tuteur,* meaning "trainer," this framework usually resembles a skeletal obelisk or pyramid. Its height and girth should be proportionate to the size and weight of the plant or plants that will scale it. Ready-made versions are available at garden centers; homemade tuteurs can be built from wood precut at a lumber yard. For strength and durability, use natural cedar or pressure-treated, knot-free lumber. The corner posts should have mitered ends, which can be aligned to form a peak. Cross braces stabilize the pyramid. The edges of the frame can be sanded down or left as is, making it easier for slender vines like morning glory and hyacinth bean to grip. If you want to apply an all-weather stain or paint, do so before any planting starts to climb.

Pot-size trellis (bottom left): Ivies and other climbing houseplants will happily grip miniature rustic arches made from willow shoots or lengths of dried grapevine. Push one end of the flexible woody support into the potting mix, close to the edge of the pot; then bend the wood until its free end can be pushed into the mix on the opposite side of the pot, anchoring it firmly.

setting up bamboo staking

In any garden where tall perennials and annuals are part of the picture, bamboo stakes probably play a key supporting role. Like most staking materials, bamboo comes in various lengths and thicknesses to stand up to plants of different sizes. Be sure to start any staking early, pushing the stake into the soil near the emerging plant but far enough away that it does not pierce major roots.

1 Size up what you need to stake. Bold accents, such as this 8-foot-tall *Polygonum japonicum* 'Crimson Beauty,' give a garden stylish accents, but only if giants are staked upright. Staking also protects the neighbors: Should this polygonum topple, it would smother everything within an 8-foot radius.

2 Dig holes: Five sockets made from 3-inch-wide PVC pipe are set into the ground around the polygonum's base. Extending 2 feet downward into the soil, these sockets provide a firm foundation for stakes.

3 Insert stakes: At the end of May, when the vine's rising stems begin to arch outward, the stakes are dropped into place. The footings laid down will hold the giant polygonum steady and upright through the toughest winter storm.

4 Begin weaving a "corset" with sisal twine; tie this on at a height of 4 feet. In a month, when the polygonum has reached its full height, weave a second corset about 2 feet higher up the stakes. Thread twine in and out; weave twine through the clump of polygonum stems and around the outside. The trick is to avoid making this too tight, which would constrict the still-growing stems and create weak points at which wind or rain might snap off new growth.

Defining an Edge

Just as a painting looks unfinished without a frame, so a garden looks (and is) unfinished without edging. It's with edging that you "ink in" the design, marking where one area ends and another begins, the point where ground cover meets path or border meets lawn. This has a practical utility: Edging will confine pachysandra, for example, keeping it from overrunning a flagstone walk, and it will keep weeds or turf from migrating into a flower bed. In the ever changing world of the planting bed, it is the edging that remains the constant.

Edging also serves to create a mood. In part, the effect depends on the material you choose. For continuity, one material, such as quarried slabs of bluestone, gives a classic look. Willow-shoot fencing has a rustic charm; a band of carefully set, smooth river stones lends a spare elegance to the picture. How you handle the material you select also determines its impact. Lay bricks flat and end to end, their tops flush with the soil surface, and they almost disappear from view yet still make a very effective edging—you can run the edge of a lawn mower right over them to give the lawn a neat definition without hand trimming. Using a series of materials repeated in sequence can create an informal effect and yet clearly mark transitions within the space of the garden.

Another visual consideration is the edging's height. It's not always necessary to lay edging flush with the ground. In fact, many precast pieces are meant to work as raised borders. Most scrolled, scalloped, looped, and filagreed leaf patterns ride across a base between 4 and 6 inches high and varying in thickness from $1/2$ to 2 inches wide. In antiques shops or flea markets you may even be lucky enough to find original pieces of cast-iron or terra-cotta roofing tiles that work as edging. Martha prefers to set weathered bricks on end in a dogtooth pattern in her Connecticut garden. Such raised edging doesn't simplify the mowing, but it does keep the bed's mulch from washing onto the turf, and like the fluting on a pie crust's edge, it gives a decorative finish.

While the buried base of this cast-limestone edging acts as a barrier to keep grass roots out of the bed, the rope-pattern top of the edging visually softens the line between lawn and garden. Plants such as purple basil grow out over the trim, further blurring the boundary.

laying edging

1 To plot a straight edge along an existing planting bed, push two stakes into the soil at opposite ends of the bed, and tie a string between them about 6 inches off the ground. Here, edging is being installed to protect expansive plantings from foot traffic and the lawn-mower blade.

2 With the taut staked string as a guide, use a sharpened edging spade to cut a line into the turf, a few inches out from the bed. Step firmly on the lip of the spade, and rock it from side to side before lifting the spade for the next cut. The neater the cut, the more tightly the edging material you insert later (step 6) will align with the turf.

3 Start digging a trench for the edging by removing the top layer of the cut turf with the flat end of a pick mattock or with a square-ended digging spade. To keep the lawn neat, lay a tarp nearby where you can pile up the soil dug out of the trench.

4 The size of the trench should depend on the thickness and depth of the edging to be installed, where it will lie relative to the soil line, and the depth of the footing you put under it. As you dig, remove any rocks or large stones: Besides preventing a smooth fit when you lay the edging, stones left underground can heave and fall during winter freezes and thaws, causing bumps and dips.

5 Shovel in a layer of sand, 1/2 to 1 inch thick, to lay a stable footing for the solid edging materials. Use coarse builder's sand, which drains more rapidly than sandbox or beach sand and is therefore better able to withstand extreme weather conditions. Gently tamp the sand into place, creating a smooth, level surface.

6 Lay units of edging as close together as possible atop the packed sand. For uneven-textured masonry edging, such as cobblestone, Belgian block, or quarried limestone, a rubber mallet can be used to tamp the surfaces flush. Fill any gaps between edging units with sand; a sliver of bamboo is useful for packing the sand into crevices. Sweep away extra sand with a brush or broom.

7 Finished edging like this stone ribbon, laid flush with the turf, is appropriately known as a "mowing strip." It provides a clear margin where the lawn mower can trim rough fringes off the grass without trespassing in the flower bed.

Edibles

For a cook, or the cook's family and friends, the greatest reward of a garden is the matchless flavors it provides. From heirloom fruits and vegetables to fresh herbs and exotic salad greens, home-grown produce elevates your dishes from something special to the truly extraordinary. In part, the character of your garden will dictate your selections. Most vegetable and fruit crops need at least six hours of direct sun a day, though leafy greens will grow reasonably well on a semishaded site, especially in the South or the Southwest. • The size of the garden should also influence planning. The gardener with a small plot, for instance, may choose to concentrate on herbs, since even a few plants can have a big impact on cuisine. Pumpkins, especially some of the fine-flavored European cultivars, such as the French heirloom 'Rouge Vif d'Etampes,' return a generous reward for a modest input of work, which makes them a great choice—if your garden is a large one. For a single pumpkin plant handily fills a whole bed.

Beans and cucumbers, the payoff of high summer, scramble up trellises in Martha's Turkey Hill vegetable garden. These trellises work in two ways: Not only do they make harvesting easier, they also save space, allowing for more of the vegetable bed to be planted out. This makes more room for companion plantings of annual salvias and marigolds that can ward off garden pests.

Menu Planning

To get the most benefit from your kitchen garden, you have to begin "menu" planning well ahead of time. You actually choose your ingredients when you design the vegetable garden. Besides satisfying your culinary requirements, menu planning is also a matter of juggling the seasons, with each one bringing a different course from the same beds, if you manage the garden skillfully.

Salad greens—arugula, say, and all those wonderful lettuces you'll never find in a supermarket—are fast grow- ing and thrive in cool weather. Planted as an early-spring crop, they'll be out of the garden and in the salad bowl by the time you are ready to plant pep- pers and other warm-weather crops. And when fall's cool weather finishes that harvest, you can replant with gar- lic, which will spread its roots and fatten its bulbs right through the win- ter, even in a Northern garden.

Aside from changing the planting scheme from season to season, you should also change it from year to year. Nearly every vegetable attracts its own pests and diseases. Growing a crop on the same piece of ground year after year gives its enemies the per- fect opportunity to settle in. The result is a serious pest-control problem.

Reconciling all of these different schedules and growth patterns in a single garden may seem intimidat- ing, but relax. Kitchen gardening is like cooking. When you first tied on an apron, you began with the simplest recipes. So, too, if you are a beginner in the garden: Plant a row of greens, a tomato plant, and a clump of basil. Then, over the freshest salads you've ever enjoyed, you can plot the next step.

fresh flavor

Tomatoes are one of the easiest and most fruitful vegetables to grow. Cherry tomatoes, like these 'Principe Borghese,' can be started indoors in late March; they bear fruit by mid July. For the best flavor, space the young plants twelve to twenty-four inches apart, give them full sun, and keep the soil even.

Arugula See Salad Greens, page 76.

Asparagus
Asparagus officinalis

Perennial

Sun *full*

Soil *organic-rich, well-drained loam, neutral (7.0) to slightly acidic pH*

Space/Thin To *18" apart in rows at least 18" apart*

Typically, asparagus takes two years from planting to yield the first cutting of spears. Once in production, however, a well-planted, well-cared-for bed will continue to bear a 6- to 8-week harvest every spring for decades.

Start Prepare soil as early in spring as it can be worked in the North and in early fall in the South. Dig trenches 12 inches deep and 18 inches across; space them 18 inches or more apart, center to center. Mix the excavated soil with well-aged compost; set it aside. Loosen the soil below the trench an additional 10 inches, and apply balanced fertilizer (the equivalent of a 10-10-10 N-P-K ratio) according to the package directions. Add 5 pounds of rock phosphate or calcium phosphate per 100 square feet, and lime as indicated by a soil-pH test. Then spread a 4-inch layer of aged compost in the trench, rake it smooth, and firm it down by walking on it. The surface should be

6 to 8 inches below grade. Add compost; refirm if it's any lower.

Set the dormant crowns in the trench, 18 to 24 inches apart, spreading out the roots. Plan on a dozen plants per adult family member. Return enough of the excavated soil to the trench to bury the asparagus roots 2 inches deep. Water the row thoroughly; water again weekly during dry weather for the rest of the first growing season. As shoots grow up from the buried crowns, shovel in more soil gradually until, by season's end, the trench is completely filled in.

Plant all-male asparagus hybrids for the biggest harvests. 'Jersey King' is best adapted to desert zones and the Southeast, 'Greenwich' to the Northeast, 'Jersey General' to the Middle Atlantic states.

Grow Weed conscientiously, but don't hoe or cultivate beds. Top dress with 2 inches of compost in fall. When stems and foliage have gone completely brown in fall or winter, mow them to the ground. Fertilize with a balanced fertilizer; apply half in early spring and half after the harvest ends, usually in June.

Harvest Pick when spears are 8 inches tall and at least ½ inch wide. Snap just below or at the soil's surface.

Pests and Problems The new all-male cultivars—strains that produce no female plants so plants won't waste time on seed production—are resist-

ant to two common diseases: rust and fusarium. Purple spot disease, which is less common, may warrant application of a chemical fungicide; control asparagus beetles by hand-picking, floating row covers, or rotenone (an insecticide made from tropical plants).

Beans
Phaseolus vulgaris

Annual

Sun *full*

Soil *organic-rich, fertile, well-drained, neutral pH*

Space/Thin To *4" to 6" apart*

If you think beans are boring, you've never grown your own and tapped into the dozens of colorful and flavorful varieties of shelling, snap, and drying beans. Particularly intriguing are the many heirloom varieties, such as the spotted 'Jacob's Cattle' and 'Vermont Cranberry' beans.

Start Sow directly into garden 2 weeks after danger of frost is past

and soil has warmed. Treat seeds with legume inoculant (available at garden centers) before sowing, and plant 1 inch deep, 2 to 3 inches apart in rows 3 to 4 feet apart. Germinates in 7 to 14 days.

Grow Mulch young plants to preserve soil moisture. Provide climbing "pole" bean cultivars with tepees of 8-foot stakes or trellises of stakes and strings.

Harvest Snap bean pods before seeds bulge. Pick shell beans when pods are fully mature and bulging with seeds, but before pods dry. For dried beans, leave pods until plants turn brown and lose most leaves—but pick before cold weather damages seeds.

Pests and Problems Move bean plantings to a new spot in four-year rotations to prevent the build-up of diseases and pests in the soil. Floating row covers help protect against Mexican bean beetle. Working among beans while their foliage is wet may spread the spores of fungal diseases from plant to plant.

Beets
Beta vulgaris

Annual

Sun *full*

Soil *organic-rich, neutral pH, well-drained; should be loose and rock-free to a depth of 8" to 9"*

Space/Thin To *4" to 6" apart*

Relatives of spinach and chard, beets yield a double harvest: sweet, slightly earthy roots and tangy greens. Thinly slice roots, and toss with arugula in a vinegar-and-oil dressing, or season roots with olive oil, salt, pepper, and rosemary, then roast in a hot oven until fork-tender. Steam or boil greens. Traditionally, beet roots are crimson, but those of some cultivars may be white or golden.

Start From upper South northward, sow directly into garden bed 2 to 3 weeks before last spring frost. In zones 8 through 10, grow as a winter or spring crop. Beets don't tolerate transplanting; do not start indoors in pots. Sow seeds 1/2 inch deep, 2 to 3 inches apart in rows 18 to 24 inches apart. Germinates in 10 to 14 days.

Grow Beets are heavy feeders, so enrich soil in which they are grown with plenty of well-aged manure. Seedlings commonly emerge in clusters; when 1 to 2 inches tall, thin by pinching off all but strongest one. Apply mulch, and water regularly to keep soil evenly moist.

Harvest Gather while young for the best-flavored greens and roots.

Pests and Problems Stunted plants are a common symptom of acidic soil—add lime as indicated by a soil test to bring pH up to 7.0.

Brassicas
Brassica juncea, B. oleracea, B. rapa

Annual

Sun *full*

Soil *organic-rich, fertile, well-drained; dig in an inch of well-aged manure before planting*

Vegetables of this group are more familiar under their individual names: broccoli, brussels sprouts, cabbage, cauliflower, Chinese cabbage, collards, kale, kohlrabi, mustard greens, and turnips. Indeed, this one genus seems to embody all of ethnic cuisine, and small wonder: Countryfolk around the world know that their brassicas can be depended on for cold hardiness and for nutritiousness. All the brassicas flourish in cool weather. In most areas it is possible to raise both a spring and fall crop, though in the Deep South (zones 8 to 10) brassicas are best reserved for a winter crop. Brassicas develop the sweetest flavor after exposure to a few fall frosts. All are flush with vitamins (mostly A and C), and some contain anticarcinogens.

Broccoli For spring crop, start seeds indoors, planting 1/4 inch deep, 5 to 7 weeks before last frost. Transplant into garden 3 to 4 weeks before last frost, setting plants 12 to 18 inches apart in rows 20 to 36 inches apart. Where summers are cool, sow directly into garden around mid May. Plant 2 to 5 seeds per foot of row, thin seedlings when 4 inches tall to spacing of 12 to 18 inches. For fall crops, sow directly into garden 85 days before first fall frost. Fertilize 3 weeks after setting out transplants, 5 weeks after sowing, applying 1 tablespoon of balanced fertilizer such as 5-10-10 per plant. Mulch, and water well. Cut heads while deep green, before buds start to open.

Brussels Sprouts In North, start seeds indoors 90 to 100 days before last fall frost, planting $1/4$ inch deep. Transplant to garden 4 to 6 weeks later, spacing 14 to 24 inches apart. In South, a spring crop is also possible if you sow directly into garden in late winter. Plant 4 to 5 seeds per foot of row, and when seedlings are 4 to 5 inches tall thin to 14- to 24-inch spacing. Fertilize monthly with balanced fertilizer such as 5-10-10 at a rate of 1 tablespoon per plant. Mulch, and water well. When each sprout reaches about half harvestable size, snap off leaf below it to give it room to grow. Sprouts ripen from bottom of stalk upward; they develop best flavor after first fall frost.

Cabbage, Chinese Cabbage For spring cabbage crop, start seeds indoors 50 to 60 days before last spring frost. Plant $1/2$ inch deep; keep seedlings cool (55 to 65 degrees). Transplant into garden 2 to 3 weeks before last frost, spacing 15 to 18 inches apart in rows 24 to 30 inches apart. For fall crop, sow seeds di-

rectly into garden, $1^1/2$ to 2 inches apart for cabbages, 3 inches apart for Chinese cabbage. When seedlings are 4 to 5 inches tall, thin cabbages to spacing of 18 to 24 inches, Chinese cabbage to 12 to 15 inches. Fertilize at same time, applying 1 pound of balanced fertilizer (5-10-10) per 25-foot row of cabbages, $1/2$ pound per 25-foot row of Chinese cabbages. Mulch cabbages and Chinese cabbages, and water well. Harvest fall crops before first fall frost, and store in cool but frost-free and moist spot such as a garage or basement.

Cauliflower Start seeds indoors in peat pots or pellets, sowing $1/4$ inch deep, 4 weeks before last spring frost. Set out in garden after all danger of frost is past, spacing plants 18 inches apart in rows 3 feet apart. For fall crop, sow directly into garden just after last spring frost, planting two seeds every 18 inches in usual rows. If both seeds germinate, snip off weaker seedling. Mulch, and water well. Cut off heads while still smooth and flower buds are small.

Collards, Kale, Mustard Greens Sow directly into garden. Plant collards 4 to 5 weeks before last spring frost, planting seeds $1/4$ inch to $1/2$ inch deep, 4 to 5 seeds per foot, in rows 3 feet apart. Thin to 6- to 12-inch spacing. Sow again in midsummer in North or late summer in South for fall crop. Sow kale in early to midsummer for fall crop, planting seeds $1/4$ inch to $1/2$ inch deep, 3 to 4 seeds per foot, in rows 18 inches apart. Thin to 8- to 12-inch spacing. Sow mustard greens 3 weeks before last spring frost, planting $1/2$ inch deep, 3 to 4 seeds per foot,

in rows 12 to 15 inches apart. Mulch, and water well. Harvest individual leaves. Don't cut central bud of kale, and plants will continue to produce well into winter. Young collards and mustard have the best flavor.

Kohlrabi The swollen, bulblike base of the stem is this fast-growing plant's harvest. Start seeds indoors, 7 to 8 weeks before last spring frost. Grow cool; transplant seedlings into garden beds 3 to 4 weeks before last frost date, spacing them 6 inches apart. Mulch, and keep well watered. Harvest by pulling up entire plant and trimming off roots and leaves.

Turnips Sow directly into garden beds as soon as soil can be worked in spring or in late summer in the North and early fall in the South. Broadcast seeds over well-prepared bed, and rake to cover to depth of $1/2$ inch. Thin seedlings to stand 4 inches apart. Mulch, and water well; harvest fall crops before ground freezes, and store roots in cool but frost-free place.

Pests and Problems Covering young plants with floating row covers protects them against cabbage maggots, flea beetle, and other pests—but remove covers from spring plantings when weather warms. Don't plant in soil where the same or another brassica grew last year, so that pests and diseases don't become entrenched.

Broccoli See Brassicas, page 66.

Brussels Sprouts See Brassicas, page 66.

Cabbage See Brassicas, page 66.

Carrots
Daucus carota

Annual

Sun *full*

Soil *light, well-drained, compost-enriched. For long-rooted types, bed should be loose and rock-free to depth of 6 to 9 inches; on heavy soils, plant short-rooted cultivars such as 'Thumbelina'*

Space/Thin To *2" to 3" apart*

Fresh carrots are delicious raw, cooked, or juiced.

Start Seed directly into garden. In cold-winter regions, sow 1 to 2 weeks before the last spring frost; continue until early summer. Make small plantings every three weeks. Sow again in mid- to late July. In zones 8 to 10, sow from June through December. Soak seeds 6 hours before sowing, and plant 1/4 inch deep, 3 to the inch in rows 12 inches apart. Germination varies, taking as long as 2 weeks.

Grow Thin when greens are a few inches tall, leaving one carrot every 2 to 3 inches. When foliage is several inches high, mulch to keep soil evenly

moist and keep roots from cracking.

Harvest Pick on cooler days when the soil is relatively dry. Lightly brush soil off roots, but don't scrub, as abrasion promotes spoilage. Snap off greens without damaging the crown, and store roots in bucket of slightly moistened sand, covering entirely except crowns. Keep bucket in cool but frost-free room with some humidity such as an unheated basement or garage.

Pests and Problems Forked roots, which can be hard to pare, result from encounters with rocks and clay.

Cauliflower See Brassicas, page 66.

Celeriac See Root Vegetables, page 76.

Chervil See Salad Greens, page 76.

Collards See Brassicas, page 66.

Corn
Zea Mays

Annual

Sun *full*

Soil *light, well-drained, fertile*

Space/Thin To *12" apart, in rows 3 to 4 feet apart*

Nothing tastes as good as ears picked at the peak of ripeness and plunged right into boiling water.

Start Begin planting as soon as danger of frost is past and the soil has warmed; make a new sowing every 2 weeks until early summer. Sow

directly into garden, planting seeds 1 inch deep, 3 to 4 inches apart. Germination time: 5 to 7 days.

Grow For best pollination, plant in 4-by-4-foot blocks rather than long rows. Provide at least 1 inch of water during dry weather, and feed with nitrogen-rich fertilizer when plants reach 8 to 10 inches and again when silks emerge from ears.

Harvest Pick ears when a pierced kernel oozes milky liquid.

Pests and Problems Many. Rotate plantings. Surround and cover with plastic bird netting to discourage raccoons and squirrels. To control corn earworms, put a few drops of mineral oil into the top of each ear after silks wilt and start to brown.

Cucumbers
Cucumis sativus

Annual

Sun *full*

Soil *organic-rich, fertile, well-drained*

Space/Thin To *18" apart if trellised; or in hills every 3 feet in rows 3 feet apart, several plants in each hill*

Cucumbers offer more variety than you might think, what with spherical yellow "lemon" cultivars and sweet Armenian types up to 18 inches long. Easy to grow. A single, well-tended plant can yield 30 to 40 pounds of vegetables.

The vegetable garden is one place to disregard formality and let your favorite edibles and flowers freely mix. The classic French example, called a potager, is better known in America as a kitchen garden. Regardless of which name you use, the idea of a loose mix of plants in a single plot creates a lush, informal beauty.

Start Sow seeds indoors in large peat pots 2 to 3 weeks before the last frost; or sow directly into garden bed 7 to 10 days after the last frost. Sow seeds ¹/₂ to 1 inch deep. Plant 4 to 5 seeds in a circle, or "hill," 12 inches across. Germinates in 7 to 14 days.
Grow Dig plenty of compost into soil before planting. Growing plants up trellises saves space. When letting plants sprawl, thin hills to two plants each when seedlings have 2 or 3 leaves. Fertilize cucumbers 4 weeks after planting by sprinkling two handfuls of compost or a tablespoon of 5-10-10 fertilizer around each plant.
Pests and Problems Row covers protect against cucumber beetles and unexpected cool weather. When flowers first appear, remove row covers so bees can pollinate the plants.

Eggplant
Solanum melongena

Annual
Sun *full*
Soil *organic-rich, fertile, well-drained*
Space/Thin To *18" to 24" apart in rows 3 to 4 feet apart*

Eggplants crave sun and warmth; in northern regions where spring is slow to arrive, try warming the soil by covering beds with sheets of black plastic before setting out plants. Northern gardeners should also explore early-maturing cultivars.
Start Sow indoors, 6 weeks before last frost. Plant seeds ¹/₄ to ¹/₂ inch deep. Move successively up to 4-inch pots. Transplant into garden 2 weeks after last frost. Germinates in 7 to 10 days.
Grow Enrich beds with plenty of well-aged manure and compost before setting out plants. Mulch about 4 weeks after transplanting, and give an inch of water a week during rainless weather. To hasten bearing, Northern gardeners should pinch off suckers that emerge from bases of bottom 3 to 4 leaf stems.
Harvest Fruits have better texture and flavor if picked when no more than half grown.
Pests and Problems A floating row cover protects vulnerable young plants from insects and unexpected cool weather. Remove the cover when the plants are well established, having reached a height of about 1 foot.

Garlic
Allium sativum

Perennial grown as biennial
Sun *full*
Soil *organic-rich, well-drained*
Space/Thin To *6" apart in rows 6" apart*

Garlic-hating vampires may not worry you, but the bulb is equally effective at warding off colds, and it seems to help in reducing blood cholesterol levels and controlling hypertension. Experiment with exotic cultivars such as purple-striped 'Chesnok Red' or the silverskin garlic 'Mild French.' Easy to grow, they are delicious as a seasoning or roasted whole and served as a surprisingly sweet, mellow vegetable in their own right.
Start Plant in fall, about 6 weeks before hard frost. Set large, firm individual cloves point up in well-prepared soil, burying cloves an inch or two below ground level in mild zones, and at twice that depth in cold-winter areas. "Softneck" types perform better in warm-weather regions and in less than ideal soils; "hardnecks," which have a more complex flavor, are better for cold zones.

Grow Mulch as soon as ground freezes. Keep area weeded and watered. Avoid use of chemical fertilizers: Excessive nitrogen promotes decay-prone bulbs. Snip off any flower shoots that appear.

Harvest Stop watering when top growth starts to yellow, usually in July, and let plants dry for a couple of weeks. Dig carefully to extract bulbs without damaging papery skins. Brush off soil, and cure for 2 to 4 weeks on a screen in a warm, dark, dry area. Afterward, trim tops and roots to within 1/2 inch of bulb, and store in a cool, dry place.

Pests and Problems Diseases are commonly a symptom of poorly drained soil; where that is a problem, plant garlic in raised beds.

Herbs

Annuals and Perennials

Sun *full sun is usually best, though broad-leaved herbs such as basil prefer partial shade in hot-summer regions*
Soil *well-drained loam, average fertility*

Ounce for ounce, even pinch for pinch, no other crop energizes your cooking like fresh-cut herbs. Certainly, no other crop is so easy to grow. Most of the traditional herbal favorites are native to dry regions with poor soils such as the hills overlooking the Mediterranean; these plants are tough and undemanding. They are naturally tolerant of drought and poor soils. Indeed, generous fertilization is likely to incite overly lush, less flavorful growth. In addition, herbs are naturally pest-resistant. Botanists believe that the powerful fragrances and flavors that pique our appetites actually evolved as a deterrent to plant-eating animals—delicious in small quantities, they upset the digestion if taken as a main course.

Start Grow from rooted cuttings or seedlings purchased at a reliable garden center. Most herbs are slow to start from seed, and homegrown seedlings usually lack decorative aspects of the named clones. Seedling rosemaries, for instance, are unlikely to have the creeping growth of 'Prostratus,' or seedling thymes the silver variegated leaves of 'Argenteus.'

Incorporate plenty of coarse sand and a moderate amount of compost (25 percent of the bed's total volume) into heavy, compacted soils. Very sandy soils also benefit from the addition of compost. But avoid over-enriching the soil with manures and large doses of fertilizer. On poorly drained sites, construct a raised bed (see page 27); a raised bed also helps protect herbs from the excessive humidity of southeastern summers. Herbs adapt well to cultivation in pots and will thrive in a sunny window or window box. They do well in rock gardens and make attractive ground covers for sunny slopes.

Plant out cold-hardy herbs such as common thyme or parsley in early spring. Delay setting out cold-sensitive herbs such as rosemary and basil until all danger of frost is past.

Grow Water new plantings regularly. Once established, most herbs thrive on the natural budget of rainfall, except in truly arid climates such as those found in the Southwest, where deep weekly irrigations are a necessity. Tropical herbs such as ginger and lemongrass are an exception to this rule; they invariably require generous irrigation.

Feed herbs in early spring with some balanced organic fertilizer (applying as recommended on the product label) or a top-dressing with compost. Where herbs such as lavender, thyme, and rosemary survive from year to year as perennials, forming woody shrubs, they will benefit from periodic shearings or prunings. Cutting back will help them maintain a compact shape and force out more flavorful, fragrant new growth.

Pests and Problems Fungal diseases may attack herb foliage on humid or poorly drained sites. Increase air flow around the plants, or move to a raised bed or containers. Insect infestations are often symptoms of over-generous watering or fertilization. Treat pests with insecticidal soap sprays or pyrethrum-based insecticides, which, if used according to the instructions on the product label, are nontoxic to humans.

Kale See Brassicas, page 66.

Kohlrabi See Brassicas, page 66.

Lettuce See Salad Greens, page 76.

Mâche See Salad Greens, page 76.

Melons, Pumpkins, and Squash
Cucumis melo, Citrullus, Cucurbita spp.

Annuals and Perennials
Sun *full*
Soil *organic-rich, fertile, loose and well-drained*

These crops seem alike: Under a hard shell lurks a soft center of sweet moist flesh. But melons, despite their bulk, are ephemeral fruits that should be picked at the moment of ripeness and eaten immediately. Pumpkins and squashes, by contrast, are like money in the bank. While summer squashes such as zucchini have only an ordinary shelf life, the thicker-shelled pumpkins and winter squashes such as 'Acorn' and 'Blue Hubbard' can rest in a cool basement for weeks without losing any of the flavor they deliver when baked and buttered.

Start These plants need a long, warm growing season, rich soil, and full sun. In the North, a gentle south-facing slope is ideal, or cover the planting area with a heat-trapping mulch of black plastic. To enrich soil, dig in a couple of inches of well-aged manure and ¹/₂ cup bonemeal per foot of row.

In the South, sow seeds directly into the garden 2 weeks after the average date of the last frost. In the North, start seeds indoors in 3-inch peat pots 3 to 4 weeks before transplanting into the garden 2 weeks after the last frost. Plant cantaloupes and other small- to medium-sized melon seeds 1 inch deep in "hills," foot-wide circles of 6 seeds, 4 to 6 feet apart. After germination thin each hill to two most vigorous plants. Set trans-

plants in two-plant hills at a similar spacing. Space watermelon hills 6 to 8 feet apart, summer-squash hills 3 feet apart in rows 4 to 6 feet apart, and winter squash and pumpkin hills 3 feet apart in rows 6 to 8 feet apart.

Grow Keep soil evenly moist; apply 1 inch of water weekly in dry weather, or as much as 2 to 3 inches in hot, dry regions. Mulch once soil has warmed.

Harvest Pick melons when fully ripe—fruits develop sweet fragrance and a crack develops where stem attaches so fruits slip off vine with little effort. A watermelon's skin turns dull and resists piercing by a fingernail. Summer squashes should be picked while small and tender for best flavor. With winter squash, wait until vine withers in the fall or frost threatens; let fruits fully ripen but move inside before exposed to freezing temperatures.

Pests and Problems Protect young plants from beetles by covering with floating row covers; remove covers when flowers open to allow pollination; replace for a period of two weeks when wild chicory first blooms to protect against squash vine borers.

Tomatoes, peppers, eggplants, and beans are among the most prolific vegetables in the garden. They thrive in full sun, rich soil, and warm temperatures. The only thing more appealing than the homegrown flavor is the colors—from rich purple-black, brilliant orange, full red, and streaked scarlet to exquisite creamy white.

Mizuna See Salad Greens, page 76.

Mustard Greens See Brassicas, page 66.

Parsley Root See Root Vegetables, page 76.

Parsnips See Root Vegetables, p. 76.

Peas

Pisum sativum, P. sativum var. *macrocarpon*

Annual

Sun *full*

Soil *light, well-drained*

Space/Thin To *2" to 3" apart*

Separating green peas from their pods is slow work, but because their flavor quickly fades, homegrown peas taste immeasurably better than those in the supermarket. Snow peas and snap-pea pods may be steamed or stir-fried whole, though in a house with children, the sweet, crunchy pods are unlikely to last the trip from garden to kitchen.

Start Treat seeds with legume inoculant (obtainable at most garden centers), and sow directly into garden, 1 inch deep, 2 to 3 inches apart in rows 18 to 24 inches apart. Sow as soon as the ground can be worked in the spring, 4 to 6 weeks before the last frost. Also good for fall plantings (see "Second Sowings," page 82). Germination time: 7 to 10 days.

Grow On heavy soil, grow in raised beds to keep seeds from rotting. Where soil is sandy, and for fall plantings, protect seeds from heat by planting in trenches 4 inches deep and 5 to 6 inches wide. When peas have reached a height of 5 to 6 inches, half-fill trench with soil; a week later, fill trench completely. Tuck in fall plantings with 4 inches of hay mulch to extend harvest. Support bush-type peas with brushwood (see "Supports," page 57) and tall cultivars with trellises of 8-foot stakes and strings.

Harvest Pick pods daily to encourage continued production.

Pests Aphids may attack vines—wash them with a strong jet of water. Handpick slugs or trap in dishes of beer set with lip almost flush with soil surface.

Peppers

Capsicum annuum

Annual

Sun *full*

Soil *fertile, well-drained*

Space/Thin To *18" to 24" apart in rows 2 to 3 feet apart*

No vegetable has the same impact on your cuisine as hot peppers, and growing your own sweet peppers opens up a pantry-full of colorful and flavorful options. The pungency or heat level of peppers is measured by Scoville Heat Units, in a scale that ranges from 0 (green bell pepper) to over 300,000 (habañero).

Start Sow seeds indoors, $1/4$ to $1/2$ inch deep, 8 to 10 weeks before last frost. Seeds germinate best at 75 to 80 degrees. Transplant into garden 2 weeks after last frost. Germination time: 7 to 10 days.

Grow Peppers originated in hot, semi-tropical regions, and plants shouldn't be moved out into the garden until nighttime temperatures remain above 55 degrees. After transplanting, remove the first blossoms before the fruit sets. This encourages the plant to establish a healthy root system before it has to support fruit. A more vigorous plant will be a heavier producer over the season. **Harvest** As fruits reach a usable size; steady picking encourages the production of more fruits. Wear gloves when picking hot peppers; the capsaicin that gives them their bite is a skin irritant. To dry hot peppers, pick when they have turned red or orange, string together with a needle and packthread, and hang up in a warm, airy spot. **Pests and Problems** Rotate plantings to keep diseases from becoming endemic in your soil; don't plant peppers or their relatives the tomatoes, potatoes, and eggplants in a spot where any of these plants have grown in the past 3 to 4 years.

Potatoes

Solanum tuberosum

Perennials

Sun *full*

Soil *well-drained, loose, slightly to moderately acidic; enrich with well-aged manure but avoid use of fresh manures or high-nitrogen chemical fertilizers, which promote leaf growth at the expense of tuber production*

Space/Thin To *12" apart in rows 3 feet apart*

If you think the only choice in potatoes is baked or mashed, then you should try growing your own. Few crops are as easy, adaptable, and productive, and home growing can put everything on your table from blue potatoes to candy-striped, as well as tubers with a naturally buttery flavor or an earthy tang.

Start In the North, plant early-season cultivars 3 to 4 weeks before the last spring frost, mid- and late-season potatoes 4 to 5 weeks later. In the South, plant early potatoes in January or February; mid- and late-season a week or two later. Cut seed potatoes into pieces as big as large ice cubes, with 2 to 3 eyes (dormant buds) each. Lay pieces on a sheet of newspaper in a well-lit, well-ventilated, and warm (70 degrees) place for twenty-four hours to let them callus. Lay out seed pieces 12 inches apart in trenches 6 to 8 inches deep and wide, and 3 feet apart in a well-prepared bed. Cover seed potatoes with 4 inches of soil.

Grow When shoots reach a height of 6 to 8 inches, pull soil into trench to fill all but top 2 inches. Hill up soil around potatoes again 2 to 3 weeks later. Mulch with straw to protect against weeds and drought. **Harvest** Hand dig a small harvest of new potatoes 8 weeks after planting; 2 weeks after the potato vines wither in late summer, dig main harvest with a spading fork, starting a foot from the main stem and working in to avoid injuring tubers. **Pests and Problems** Leafhoppers, tiny grasshopper look-alikes, stunt the leaves and spread viral diseases. Spray infested plants with insecticidal soap or with nonpersistent botanically derived insecticides such as sabadilla, pyrethrum, or ryania. Rotenone 5 percent and pyrethrum are effective controls for blister beetles and Colorado potato beetles, which if unchecked can defoliate potato plants. In rainy areas, buy small seed potatoes that measure no more than 2 inches in diameter—"B" tubers—and plant them whole. This reduces the danger of the seed's rotting before it sprouts.

Root Vegetables

Celeriac, parsley root, parsnip, salsify, winter radish

Annuals and biennials grown as annuals

Sun *full*

Soil *light, loose, well-drained*

Though rarely seen in American gardens, these old-world favorites offer delicate flavors and lots of nutrition with little cost in calories. Because their roots are sweetened by exposure to cool weather, they make good candidates for chilly climates.

Celeriac *(Apium graveolens* var. *rapaceum)* A close relative of celery, this root crop has a similar, though more assertive, flavor. In the North and upper South, start seeds indoors 8 to 12 weeks before last spring frost, and transplant into a raised bed enriched with aged manure or compost when 2 to $2^{1}/_{2}$ inches high. In zones 8 to 10, sow the seeds into a semishaded nursery bed, and transplant seedlings to a sunny raised bed when weather cools in fall. Space transplants 6 to 12 inches; keep well watered and mulched. Harvest when roots are 3 to 4 inches in diameter; grate raw into salads.

Parsley Root *(Petroselinum crispum* var. *tuberosum)* A close relative of leaf parsley, this root has a potent, nutty flavor that complements rich soups and stews. Grow like parsley, starting seeds indoors, 10 to 12 weeks before the last spring frost. To improve germination, wash seeds in mild detergent solution, rinse twice, and soak overnight in warm water before planting. Transplant into garden 2 to 3 weeks before last frost, into a deeply dug, sandy, and pebble-free bed. Set plants 12 to 14 inches apart. Mulch in late fall. Harvest as needed; roots may overwinter in the ground in milder regions.

Parsnip *(Pastinaca sativa)* This root looks like an albino carrot, but the nutty, tangy flavor is all its own. Steam, braise, and slice into stews and casseroles. Sow directly into deeply dug, compost-enriched, and stone-free garden beds, in early spring in North, and late summer in South. Plant seeds 1 inch apart in rows 12 to 18 inches apart, and cover with $^{1}/_{8}$ inch of sand. Cover rows with boards in late-summer plantings, and take care that seeds beneath stay moist. Germination may take 3 to 4 weeks. Thin seedlings to 3 to 6 inches apart, and keep soil evenly moist. Feed monthly with a cup of balanced fertilizer such as 5-10-10 per 25 feet of row.

Salsify *(Tragopogon porrifolius)* Also known as "vegetable oyster," this root really does taste like something you'd find on a half-shell, and is highly prized by gourmets. Grow like parsnips, planting seeds 2 inches apart and $^{1}/_{4}$ inch deep in rows 3 feet apart. Thin seedlings to a spacing of 4 to 6 inches.

Winter Radish *(Raphanus sativus* var. *longipinnatus)* An essential ingredient of many Asian cuisines, winter radishes are eaten raw and pickled, as in Korean kimchi, and cooked in stir-fries and soups. Sow directly into garden beds, in early to midsummer in the North and early fall in the South. Plant seeds $^{1}/_{2}$ inch deep, 2 to 3 inches apart, in rows 12 inches apart. Thin seedlings to stand 4 to 5 inches apart. Keep soil evenly moist. Store harvested roots as with carrots.

Salad Greens

Arugula, chervil, lettuce, mâche, mizuna, spinach

Sun *full or semi-shade*

Soil *organic-rich, fertile, well-drained loam*

Salads are fundamental to a healthy diet, and a basic part of any well-balanced meal. Fresh greens make the difference between a salad that is just that and one that is an experience. Plan your planting well, and you'll be harvesting these crisp, crunchy crops year-round. Because the flavor and texture of the new leaves is best, avoid planting any salad crop all at once. Instead, make small but repeated sowings at intervals of 2 to 3 weeks, to ensure a regular supply of tender baby leaves.

Arugula *(Eruca vesicaria* ssp. *sativa)* An ethnic specialty only a few years ago, this fast-growing green with a peppery, nutty flavor has taken our salad bowls by storm. Sow seeds directly into the garden in early to midspring or early fall (and on into the winter in the Deep South). Sprinkle seeds thickly in broad bands, and scratch into the soil with a hand cultivator. Keep soil evenly moist. Harvest by shearing off whole plants 2 to 3 inches above ground level, leaving central leaf bud to regrow. Frost-tolerant.

Chervil *(Anthriscus cereifolium)* Delicate, anise-flavored leaves sometimes called "French parsley." Sow directly into garden in early spring and again in late summer (or fall in mild-winter regions). Sow 6 to 8 seeds per foot in rows 9 to 12 inches apart, lightly covering seeds with soil. Thin seedlings so they stand 6 to 8 inches apart. Harvest by shearing whole plant, as with arugula. Chervil is excellent for winter harvests if planted in a cold frame (see "Building a Cold Frame," page 131); it withstands temperatures down to 0 degrees.

Lettuce *(Lactuca sativa)* The salad's foundation; sow directly into the garden, beginning as soon as the soil can be worked in spring. Continue sowing through midspring, changing types of lettuce as the weather warms. Crisphead lettuces are the least heat tolerant and should be planted earliest; follow with romaine, then butterhead, and finally looseleafs such as green oakleaf, 'Sierra,' and 'Deer Tongue.' Summer sowings are possible from the North to the upper South if started in cell packs indoors. Immediately after sowing put trays in a refrigerator for 3 to 4 days to help seeds break dormancy, then move to a window with indirect light. Transplant to garden when seedlings are 2 to 3 inches tall, and set in a semishaded spot. Return to sowing directly in garden in fall. Covering lettuces with a floating row cover will protect them from light frosts and extend the season.

Mâche *(Valerianella locusta)* Also called "corn salad," this hardy little green will overwinter where temperatures don't drop below 5 degrees, and is even more cold tolerant if protected with a straw mulch. Plant in early spring or late summer to fall. Broadcast seeds thickly in blocks or bands, and cover with $1/4$ inch of sand. Water regularly during dry weather. Pick leaves as soon as they are big enough to eat.

Mizuna *(Brassica rapa* var. *nipposinica)* A Japanese mustard that makes a cushion of feathery, mildly pungent greens. Plant in early to late spring; mizuna is very slow to bolt in hot weather and will continue to provide salads into August if kept watered. Broadcast seeds sparingly in blocks or rows, and scratch into the soil with a hand cultivator. Thin seedlings to stand 8 to 9 inches apart. Begin planting again in late summer, as mizuna is also cold-tolerant, and even in the North will grow all winter in the protection of a cold frame. Harvest by shearing as with arugula; greens are ready for cutting as early as 2 to 3 weeks after sowing.

Spinach *(Spinacia oleracea)* Throughout most of North America, sow directly into garden in early spring as soon as soil can be worked and again in late summer. In zones 9 and 10, sow in late fall for a winter crop. Plant seeds $1/2$ inch deep in rows $1 1/2$ to 2 feet apart. Thin seedlings to a spacing of 5 to 6 inches. To increase the yield, fertilize with a balanced fertilizer such as 10-10-10 at the rate specified on the product label when seedlings emerge.

Salsify See Root Vegetables, page 76.

Spinach See Salad Greens, page 76.

Tomatoes
Lycopersicon esculentum

Annual
Sun *full*
Soil *rich, fertile, well-drained*
Space/Thin To *For indeterminate tomatoes, plant 24" apart in rows 30" apart if on trellises; every 30" in rows 36" apart if sprawling. For determinate tomatoes, plant every 30" in rows 30" apart.*

Selecting the right tomato for your region is crucial to success. Check the estimated "days to maturity" listed on the plant label or seed packet. This interval may range from 50 days to almost 100; fast-maturing types are better for Northern gardens. The letters sometimes listed on labels or in catalogs after a tomato's name—V,F,N, and T—indicate resistance to various common diseases, such as verticillium wilt and fusarium.

Tomatoes also fall into two categories, "indeterminate" and "determinate." Indeterminate cultivars continue to grow throughout the warm weather, bearing fruit in a gradual stream, an ideal situation for those who want just a fruit or two at a time for a salad or sandwich. Determinate cultivars stop growing when plants mature and bear the bulk of their fruits all at once, making them more convenient for sauce-makers and home canners.

Start Sow indoors 4 to 6 weeks before the last frost; plant seeds ¼ inch deep. Transplant seedlings into larger containers as often as twice to avoid root crowding, ending up in 4-inch pots. Set outdoors 1 week after last frost. Germinates in 7 to 14 days if soil remains warm, at 70 to 80 degrees.

Grow For a stronger, healthier plant, bury a lanky tomato transplant horizontally in a trench with just the tip and a couple of sets of leaves exposed—roots will grow along the buried stem. Let the ground warm, and give the plants a chance to establish themselves before mulching, which will help the soil retain moisture and control weeds.

Without staking or pruning, indeterminate plants may expend all their energy on making new leaves and stems rather than ripening fruit. To avoid this, pinch off the small side shoots that grow where the leaf stem joins the main stem. Remove these shoots before they reach 3 inches to avoid damaging the plant. Always wash your hands first, especially if you also grow eggplant, nicotiana, petunias, potatoes, or other plants that share diseases with tomatoes. After the end of July, Northern gardeners should remove all flower clusters to focus plants on ripening existing fruits and prevent them from bearing additional ones that won't ripen before frost.

To stake, drive 6-foot stout wooden posts or metal fence posts into the ground beside the young plants, and tie up stems with cloth strips or soft twine. Place tomato "cages"— 18-inch wide cylinders of wire fencing—around shorter determinate tomato bushes to keep fruits off the ground. To use cages with indeterminates, stack the cylinders on top of each other until the required height is reached, or let the plants grow up and drape down over the side.

Pests Rotate plantings to keep diseases from becoming endemic in your soil; don't plant tomatoes or their relatives the peppers, potatoes, and eggplants in a spot where any of these plants have grown in the past 3 to 4 years. Too much heat— days above 95 degrees or nights above 75 degrees—kills the pollen and prevents flowers from setting fruit. Tomatoes will start producing again when temperatures drop.

Turnips See Brassicas, page 66.

Winter Radishes See Root Vegetables, page 76.

Planning a Vegetable Patch

The first step in creating a vegetable garden, according to traditional wisdom, lies in choosing a suitable site. In fact, in the typical suburban property of today, the site usually chooses itself. That's because vegetables have such definite needs that, commonly, only one area of the yard can fulfill all of them.

To go from a seed all the way to an arm-filling pumpkin in a matter of 3 to 4 months is quite a feat, so it's not surprising that vegetables, the athletes of the plant world, should require a specific regimen. The most important requirement is for sunlight. Most vegetables need at least 6 hours of full sunlight daily, which means that the vegetable garden must lie in an open spot away from the shade of trees. In addition, the soil must be deep, fertile, and well aerated. You can help nature by importing compost and other soil improvers, but you'll surely regret a decision to set the garden down on a rocky ledge.

A vegetable-garden soil should also be evenly moist, which means that the site should be level, so that rainfall and irrigation water soak in where they fall instead of washing down into low spots or running off downhill. However, the drainage must also be good: Selecting a site in your yard's low spot is bound to be a mistake.

Plan, too, for accessibility. Locate the garden within a short hose-length of a faucet so that watering is easy. Neglect the irrigation, and your harvest will be meager, tough, and bitter. Make sure, as well, that it's a short trip down a level path from garden to composting area. A vegetable garden has a ravenous appetite for compost, and sanitation, keeping the garden free of plant debris, is the best way to keep it free of insect pests. And consider proximity to the kitchen. Keeping the garden convenient to the kitchen door saves steps when you are picking dinner, and it encourages more frequent visits. Dropping by the garden on a regular basis will keep you posted about its ongoing needs for irrigation, weeding, staking, or spraying.

Keeping the vegetable garden close at hand, however, making it a more prominent part of the landscape, also

A good layout for your garden will take full advantage of the different vegetables' potential. Blocks of plants laid out to be accessible from any path keep feet out of the planting beds. Bamboo fencing and tripods add structure and supports for plants.

a fruitful plot

dictates a different, less purely utilitarian kind of design than the traditional, regimented rows. The *potager,* a French-inspired mixing of flowers and vegetables, has become the popular model for a more decorative style of vegetable garden, though you can also refer back to the early American "dooryard" garden. These traditions share reliance on a precise and symmetrical pattern of beds. Establishing such a formal, geometric framework emphasizes, through contrast, the planting's lushness and diversity, making the easy intermingling of vegetables, flowers, and herbs all the more appetizing. Cutting the garden into many beds also serves a practical purpose: It lets you keep crops distinct so that you can give each the care it needs without disturbing the neighbors.

Before you begin sketching plans for the garden, however, you should establish what will fit visually into your landscape. The best tool for that

is a camera. The human eye passes over details it finds displeasing. You see the scene as you wish it were. A camera, however, impartially records all the details. After you've chosen the site for the vegetable garden, stand at the various vantage points from which you'll view it—the kitchen window, the gate to the backyard, etc.—and take a series of photographs at each spot. Hold the camera level, and turn it after each shot, so that, bit by bit, it records a panoramic sweep.

When the photographs have been developed, patch each series together into a continuous ribbon, and use a color photocopier to expand the resulting strips. Then lay a sheet of tracing paper over each photocopy, and sketch the changes you propose to make. Use additional sheets of tracing paper to try beds of various sizes and shapes; experiment with different placements of trellises, arbors, and the scarecrow.

The plantings you select for the vegetable garden will depend largely on what you like to eat. But in a garden intended to be decorative as well as productive, aesthetics also play a

role in setting the planting plan. Swiss chard, for instance, may not be your favorite dish, but can you resist the contrast 'Ruby' chard's vibrant red stems make when interplanted with the white of chard 'Argentata'? And though cardoon *(Cynara cardunculus)* is, as a dish, hopelessly bland, its bold, toothed silver leaves and towering thistlelike sapphire flowers make this perennial relative of the artichoke a vegetable-garden must.

Above all, remember that meticulous scheduling is the heart of a successful vegetable garden. Peas planted a few weeks too late won't set any pods before the summer sun withers the vines. Chinese cabbages sown too late in the fall simply won't "head" before the frost cuts them down. After you have chosen the crops you want to grow, make a note of all the planting times, and work out on paper when each will be planted and where. By coordinating plantings in this manner, you can easily harvest an early crop and a late one from the same bed.

Before putting a shovel to soil, time should be spent putting pencil and pen to paper. Planning a vegetable garden should also include the organization of a tight planting schedule. Coordinating both of these will lead to a more successful, continuous harvest.

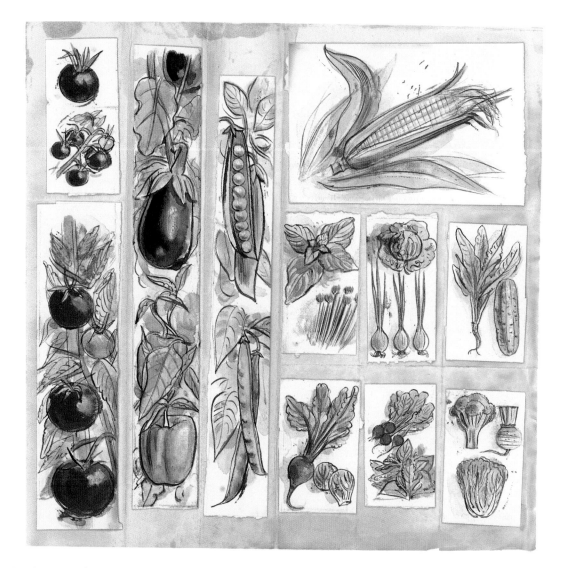

design for a kitchen garden

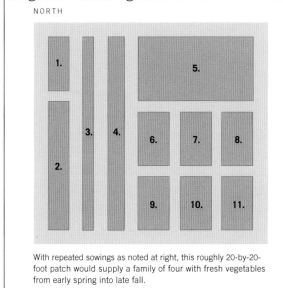

NORTH

With repeated sowings as noted at right, this roughly 20-by-20-foot patch would supply a family of four with fresh vegetables from early spring into late fall.

1. **Cherry tomatoes** Grown on wooden tepees or metal cages with other indeterminate varieties

2. **Determinate tomatoes** These are the best varieties for saucemaking and canning

3. **Eggplant** (purple and white) and **peppers** (sweet and hot)

4. **Peas** (shelling and snap) in spring; replaced by **bush beans** in summer

5. **Corn** For a steady supply, sow every 2 weeks

6. **Chives, dill, parsley, sweet basil,** and other culinary herbs

7. **Lettuce** (looseleaf for cut-and-come-again harvest), spring; **onions,** summer

8. **Spinach,** spring; **cucumbers,** summer (sow one hill)

9. **Beets, Swiss chard,** spring; **kale, brussels sprouts,** fall

10. **Radishes, carrots,** spring; **mesclun mix,** fall

11. **Cabbage** (mix small and large varieties), **cauliflower** ('Early White'), **broccoli,** spring; **collards, kale, turnips,** fall

Second Sowings

For far too many vegetable gardeners, spring is *the* planting season. When summer heat withers their pea vines and causes their lettuce to bolt, let whole beds lapse into vacant space. The real kitchen-garden veteran, though, knows that summer and fall, and in the subtropical south, winter, are planting seasons, too.

Throughout most of the Northeast and upper Midwest, as cool-weather-loving crops pass away in early summer, you can fill the vacant spots with heat-loving vegetable seedlings started indoors, such as tomatoes and squashes. Tuck these in with direct sowings of other heat-loving or heat-tolerant vegetables such as bush beans and a late sowing of carrots or corn.

Early summer is also planting time for heat-loving vegetables in coastal regions of southern California, where summers are sunny but not scorching. In the cloudy, cool Pacific Northwest, you can sow summer vegetables or start a new generation of cool-season crops. In the Deep South and much of the Southeast, summer, with its intense heat, is a dormant season in the kitchen garden. But when the weather cools again in September, the South's best season for cool-weather vegetable crops is just getting underway. Plant lettuce or broccoli, and they'll flourish in the long interval before winter. Gardeners in milder parts of the northern states, the Middle Atlantic region, and the mountain South—upland North Carolina, Tennessee, Kentucky, and West Virginia—can do the same, but they must check, before sowing, that enough days remain before the first fall frost for crops to mature.

To do this, check the "days to maturity" listed on the seed packet. Because growth tends to slow in fall, this figure should be increased by a half. By counting backward that number of days from the average date of the first fall frost, you can arrive at the sowing date for your region.

In the Deep South and the milder regions of the Southwest, mid- to late fall is a third planting season. By sowing frost-tolerant crops such as peas and cabbage, Southerners can extend their harvest through winter to spring. Northerners can sow the same crops into a cold frame.

early to midsummer sowings

Plant	Region *(see note, opposite) and Sowing Time	Notes
Beets, Swiss Chard	B: June–August	Late sowings escape spinach-leaf-miners, which commonly attack spring sowings
Beans (bush types)	A: June–July; B: June–July; C: July–August; D: July	Black-eyed peas and crowder peas are good summer beans for the Southeast
Carrots	A: June–July; B: June–August; C: June–August; D: June–August	Short-rooted cultivars such as 'Thumbelina' are faster maturing and better in the North
Corn	A: May–June; C: April–July; D: June–July; E: May–June	Early-summer sowings of sweet corn are not advised north of zone 5
Cucumbers	A: June; B: June–July; D: June	Need warm weather to germinate, but do not flourish when temperatures rise into 90s
Onions	B: June–August	Plant "long day" cultivars; "short day" cultivars turn to bulb production too soon
Tomatoes	C: June; E: June–July	Start seeds indoors; use seedlings to replace heat-killed plants after midsummer

late-summer to early-fall sowings

Plant	Sowing Time	Notes
Beans (bush type)	C: August–September; E: August–September	More tender and less stringy if grown as fall crop in the South
Cabbage (and other brassicas such as collards, kale, and turnip)	A: July–August; B: August; C: August–October; D: July–August; E: September–October	In regions A, B, and D, check days to maturity on seed packets; schedule sowings so harvest comes around or before first fall frost
Carrots	B: August; C: August–October; D: August; E: September–October	Check days to maturity on seed packets; schedule sowings so harvest comes around or before first fall frost
Cucumbers	C: August–September; E: August–September	Soak seeds overnight before planting; cover sowings with scrap lumber until germination begins
Lettuce and Spinach	A: August; B: August–September; C: August–October; D: August–September; E: September–October	In the North sow cold-hardy lettuce cultivars such as 'Arctic King'
Onions	A: August; C: September; D: August–September; E: August–October	Sow short-day cultivars in the South; hardy bunching onions where winters are severe
Peas	A: July; B: July; C: August–September; D: July	Cover to protect from early frost
Radishes (spring and winter types)	A: August–October; B: August–October; C: September–October; D: September–October; E: October	In the North, mulch winter radishes with straw after the first frost; roots will sweeten and continue to gain bulk into winter

late-fall to early-winter sowings

Plant	Sowing Time	Notes
Carrots	C: October–December; E: October–December	Protect from frost with straw mulch
Collards, Kale, Turnips	C: October–November; E: October–November	Winter harvests have sweetest flavor
Lettuce and Spinach	C: October–December; E: October–December	In zone 7, grow in a cold frame
Peas	E: November–December	Latest plantings are in Florida
Radishes	C: October–December; D: October; E: October–December	Sow winter-type radishes 90 days before fall frost; sow spring radishes until 30 days before frost

*Sowing information appears for five distinct regions—Region A: Northeast and Mid-Atlantic states, upper Midwest, and Rocky Mountain West (USDA Zones 3 to 7); Region B: Pacific Northwest (Zones 6 to 9); Region C: Southern California, Southwest (Zones 8 to 10); Region D: Mountain South: NC, TN, VA, WV, KY (Zones 6 to 7); Region E: Deep South and Hawaii (Zones 7 to 10).

Annuals, Perennials, and Bulbs

In the kitchen garden, you are a chef, but step into the rest of the landscape, and you become an artist. And when the land is your canvas, plants are your pigments. That dictates a very different kind of relationship to your ornamental plants, the annuals, perennials, and bulbs with which you decorate your landscape. To use these plants effectively, you must know how they look in different seasons and in different situations, and start forming opinions about which plants work well together, and which don't. • Of course, plants are much more than hues on a palette, and distinctions among them are less clear-cut. Often, a single plant fits into more than one category. Many plants that are perennials in the South, for example, need to be grown as annuals in the North. Even if the distinctions among plant types are somewhat artificial, though, they can be useful in alerting you to the roles that different species might play in your garden.

In spring, Martha's Turkey Hill garden is a mix of annuals, perennials, and bulbs. Under a blossoming wisteria, pansies (annuals) edge beds of tulips, muscari, and daffodils (all bulbs). Early-flowering perennials such as primroses, bleeding hearts, and pulmonarias complete the picture. With staged plantings, later-flowering annuals, perennials, and bulbs will provide color in the same beds throughout summer.

Annuals Botanists define an annual as a plant such as African marigold *(Tagetes erecta)* or common sunflower *(Helianthus annuus)* that is genetically programmed to complete its full life cycle within one year. That is, the seed germinates, and the seedling grows into a mature plant that blooms, sets seed, and afterward dies, all within the space of one growing season. In practice, however, gardeners also treat as annuals many plants that are not genetically programmed for this short life but which are actually fast-growing, frost-sensitive perennials. A plant of New Guinea impatiens, for example, persists from year to year in its tropical homeland but can't survive a North American winter. Because it blooms during its first season of growth, we grow New Guinea impatiens anyway, but as an annual.

Plant for plant, annuals generally bear more flowers than perennials and remain in bloom for a much longer period. Perennials devote much of their strength to storing the energy they need to overwinter. Annuals, on the other hand, literally bloom themselves to death, and this makes them superior for window boxes and other containers as well as the cutting garden.

Some gardeners shy away from annuals because they must be replanted every year, or even more often. Snapdragons and pansies, for example, are annuals that thrive during the cool, moist weather of spring, but which usually perish in the heat of summer, whereupon they must be replaced by more heat-tolerant plantings. In some respects, though, annuals' impermanence is an advantage. Because these plants are pulled from the bed each fall, their pests and diseases are unlikely to become entrenched as they commonly do in perennial plantings. Fast growth also makes annuals an ideal plug for the gaps that appear seasonally in perennial plantings. When your tulips retreat back underground, slip in some annuals to fill out the display until next year.

Annuals' fast growth also encourages adventurous design. A perennial border takes several years to mature, and you don't want to discover at the end of that time that your color scheme does not quite work. Try it out with annuals, though, and you'll know in weeks if it was an inspiration or a flop, and if you hate the results, simply replant.

a season of color

Zinnias are native to Mexico and warm regions of the Southwestern United States and Central and South America. Fast-growing, easy annuals in cold-winter climates, with flowers from midsummer into fall, they are dependable for cutting or for garden color.

Perennials

Hardening Off Annuals

Whether you start annual seedlings yourself or buy them from a nursery, they need conditioning before you move them into the garden. Otherwise, the transition from a controlled, indoor or greenhouse environment to the more stressful outdoors is likely to bring on a collapse.

Begin "hardening off" the seedlings by setting the packs or pots outdoors for just an hour or two, in a spot sheltered from the wind and where the sunlight is filtered by overhead branches. If it's spring, wait for a day when the temperature rises above 50 degrees.

Over the next week to ten days, increase the time you leave the seedlings outdoors each day by ½ hour to 1 hour daily. If they are sun-loving plants, gradually expose the seedlings to more intense sunlight, too. Leave seedlings indoors on chilly days, resuming the hardening off when the weather warms. By the second week's end, the seedlings should be staying out all day and night, and are ready for the move to the garden.

Any plant that persists for two or more growing seasons is a perennial, and so technically the group includes trees and shrubs as well as cacti and seaweeds. But when gardeners and nurserymen refer to perennials, what they usually mean is a herbaceous perennial, one of those garden flowers that dies back to the ground after it blooms or at the end of the growing season and sprouts anew the following spring.

Such plants have the obvious advantage of durability. Select a species that is well adapted to your site and to the local climate, start with a healthy specimen and give it good care, and you'll be enjoying its blossoms and foliage for years. Indeed, the longest-lived herbaceous perennials, such as peonies and bearded irises, may persist happily for decades.

Perhaps because perennials have long been the favored flowers of expert gardeners, they offer a more delicate, subtler kind of beauty than the general run of annuals. With perennials, you create a more sophisticated garden picture. Because the individual types of perennials pass in and out of bloom much more rapidly than annuals, to create an equally lasting floral display you must weave together many different species. But this diversity means that a perennial planting is constantly changing the character of its display, presenting a picture that evolves with the seasons and which is new and different every day.

Creating a perennial border does require a longer commitment than planting a bed of annuals. However, the durability of a perennial planting means that you can refine it over a period of years, adding to and rearranging the perennials in it until you achieve just the effect that you desire.

One virtue inexperienced gardeners often falsely attribute to perennials is that because they don't need yearly replacement they involve less work than annual flowers. In fact, to keep a perennial border in trim requires regular attention. Plants that outgrow their space must be divided, failing plants must be replaced, and weeding, watering, deadheading, and feeding must all be attended to. If taken care of on a regular basis, however, these chores shouldn't involve more than an hour or two on any one day.

Peonies rank among the most reliable and long-lived perennials a gardener can grow. After their spring blooms have faded, these low-maintenance plants' lush, dark-green foliage provides a backdrop for other flowers.

Perennials from Seed

The common route to stocking a perennial border is to buy the plants, garden-ready, in containers. However, you can also start your perennials from seed. This requires patience, as most perennials don't flower until a full year after they are sown, and many take two years or even more to reach blooming size. But by starting from seed, you can raise a gardenful of perennials for about the cost of a single potted specimen.

A perennial gardener with big plans really has to master seed starting. So does one with a taste for the exceptional—blue Himalayan poppies, say, or native Southwestern penstemons. You can purchase seeds of such rarities, but not, usually, plants.

The traditional season for planting perennial seeds comes in July, during the lull between the spring rush and fall cleanup. Sow the seeds into containers of moistened soilless potting mix; ordinary cell packs work well for this. The rule of thumb is to bury seeds to a depth equal to three times their diameter, though really fine seeds, such as those of foxgloves, are better just sprinkled over the soil's surface and left to wash in.

After sowing, moisten the soil with a gentle spray of water. Then check the seed packets to see if they recommend a period of "moist chilling"—many kinds of hardy perennial seeds won't germinate without exposure to cold. If moist chilling is recommended, seal the containers in plastic bags and store them in the refrigerator. The seed packets may offer specific recommendations about the length of chilling your seeds require. For most kinds of perennials, one to two weeks of moist chilling will suffice, but some species require as many as twelve.

After chilling, set the seed containers out in a cold frame, resting them on an inch of clean sand. Cover the containers with a piece of dampened burlap to keep the potting mix and seeds from drying out, and lay old window screens or a strip of snow fencing over the top of the frame to filter the harsh summer sun and winds. Water the containers as necessary, with a gentle spray, and peel back the burlap daily to check for germination. At the first sign of green sprouts, remove the burlap.

Thin the seedlings to one per cell by snipping off excess plants with a pair of nail scissors. Extras may also be transplanted, when they have sprouted their third or fourth adult-type leaf, into cells where seeds failed to sprout.

By early fall, the perennial seedlings should be big enough to move out of the cold frame. Husky seedlings can go right into garden beds. Plants too small to hold their own amid an established planting, however, should be nurtured in a nursery area. Some area of the vegetable garden from which you have already harvested the crop works well for this; plant the little perennials out at 6- to 10-inch intervals and blanket them with evergreen boughs through winter's freezing weather. The following year, as the plants bulk up and as you have the bed space, you can move them from the nursery to their permanent spot in the garden.

first-year-flowering perennials grown from seed

Species and Cultivar Name	Weeks from Sowing to Bloom	Hardiness (USDA Zones)*	Notes
Yarrow (Achillea millefolium) 'Colorado,' 'Summer Pastels'	17-20 weeks	Zones 3-9	Start seeds from late December to February.
Columbine (Aquilegia) 'Song Bird' series	26-32 weeks	Zones 3-9	Blooms first year.
Carpathian bellflower (Campanula carpatica) 'Uniform' series	5-18 weeks	Zones 3-7	
Coreopsis (Coreopsis grandiflora) 'Early Sunrise'	12-14 weeks	Zones 4-9	Not long-lived in South, surviving there on average 3-5 years.
Shasta daisy (Chrysanthemum x superbum) 'White Knight'	25-30 weeks	Zones 4-9	Short-lived in Southeastern gardens; need protection in North.
Delphinium (Delphinium spp.) Belladonna hybrids D. x elatum	18-22 weeks	Belladona hybrids Zones 3-7 D. x elatum Zones 2-7	D. x elatum cultivars not reliably perennial in hot, humid summers or cold, wet winters.
Maiden pink (Dianthus deltoides) 'Zing Rose'	15-20 weeks	Zones 3-8	
Purple coneflower (Echinacea purpurea) 'Magnus'	32-36 weeks	Zones 3-8	Blooms first year; display better in subsequent years.
Blanket flower (Gaillardia x grandiflora) 'Goblin'	26-30 weeks	Zones 2-9	Blooms first year; display better in subsequent years.
Common mallow (Hibiscus moscheutos) 'Disco Belle' series	14-16 weeks	Zones 5-9	Easy to grow and dependable.
Cardinal flower (Lobelia cardinalis) 'Fan' series	18-22 weeks	Zones 2-9	Needs protection of winter mulch, especially in northerly zones.
Maltese cross (Lychnis chalcedonica)	20-26 weeks	Zones 4-7	Often short-lived.
Balloon flower (Platycodon grandiflorus)	22-26 weeks	Zones 3-7	Blooms first year; display better in subsequent years.
Hybrid sage (Salvia x superba) 'Blue Queen'	22-24 weeks	Zones 5-9	Flowers well first year; better in subsequent years.
Veronica (Veronica spicata) 'Blue Banquet'	18-21 weeks	Zones 3-7	Short-lived: 2 to 3 years.

*Hardiness data from Allen M. Armitage, Herbaceous Perennial Plants (Stipes Publishing, Champaign Illinois, 1997)

Shade

Opportunity or challenge— shade is what you make of it. Throughout most of the United States, shade is a summertime pleasure for the human population, and in the South it's more or less a necessity. Yet when it comes to fitting plants into a shady site, we call it a problem.

Actually, shade is a chance to create a special kind of garden, one with a character of its own and effects to rival those of any sun-drenched border. It's also a haven for more sensitive plants. Learn how to manage shade, and you'll be seeking out the shadows cast by your house and shed, and planning for the shade of that tree, or even of that pair of large shrubs.

Impatiens and coleus have won positions of prominence in nursery sales yards as "color for the shade" and both are valuable in that respect, if terribly overused. But your shade palette needn't stop with those two pigments. You can transform a dimly lit corner with the luminous foliage of *Hosta* 'Piedmont Gold' and variegated ribbon grasses, for example; golden-splashed foliage glows in such a setting, and it appreciates the protection from direct sunlight, which can burn paler leaves.

Foliage texture is also important in waking up dark places and creating points of interest. Rather than feel cheated, the shade gardener can revel in opportunities to use such beauties as *Hakonechloa macra* 'Aureola,' a green-and-yellow-striped grass that prefers low light, or *Petasites japonicus,* an aggressive perennial that has giant leaves of almost tropical character, despite its bone-hardy cold tolerance.

The importance of foliage shouldn't cause you to dismiss shade-adapted flowers. *Corydalis flexuosa* 'Purple Leaf', for example, sprinkles itself with blue flowers in summer; and the arisaemas, the jack-in-the-pulpits, come in exotic species such as the Asian *Arisaema sikokianum,* whose white-lined hooded purple blossoms are as dramatic as the bold leaves.

Edge out into the partial shade (often called "part shade") and you'll find a host of showier flowers: columbines, foxgloves, some of the perennial geraniums (from the genus *Geranium*), and celandine poppy (*Stylophorum diphyllum*) with its golden buttercup flowers. Fine as these blooms may be, however, it's still hard to imagine any flower more beautiful than a frond of Japanese painted fern (*Athyrium goeringianum*) with its chocolate midribs and silver-flecked leaflets—a prize of the true shade.

Timing helps define the effect of shade. In the Southeast and the Southwest, shade at midday through early afternoon—the time of day when sunlight is most intense—benefits even plants that are normally categorized as sun loving. Or consider areas canopied by the branches of deciduous trees: In summertime, you would certainly describe such places as heavily shaded, and yet in early spring, before the leaves emerge, those same spots are bathed in sunlight, making them a perfect niche for narcissus, crocus, muscari, and other spring-flowering bulbs.

To fully understand the aesthetic potential of shade, take a walk in the woods and see what nature has planted there. These native Americans have become the plants of fashion in recent years, and rightly so. One only has to see a single well-grown specimen of *Trillium sessile* var. *luteum*—a yellow-flowered trillium with big, silver-dappled leaves—to understand why these woodland inhabitants command the attention of connoisseur shade gardeners in many parts of the country.

Left: The branches of a western red cedar filter light for shade-loving False Solomon's seal (Smilacina racemosa) *and trillium. Native to woodland habitats, both perennials adapt readily to gardens canopied by trees. Below: Shade gems at Heronswood Nursery, in Kingston, Washington, include* Corydalis flexuosa *'Purple Leaf,'* Rhododendron yakushimanum, *and* Ellisiophyllum pinnatum.

Before placing a shade plant, investigate how much sunlight it really needs. Top: Bunchberry (Cornus canadensis), *native to Northern forests, thrives in dense shade. Above: Foxgloves* (Digitalis purpurea) *prefer the dappled light found in high or partial shade.*

A Guide to Shade

As soon as you start searching out plants for your shady spot, you'll discover that there are many degrees of shade. Your success in planting will depend on evaluating the shade in your garden correctly and matching it to a corresponding group of plants.

High Shade Found under a high canopy of branches, typically offering bright but indirect or filtered light. Fosters a wide range of plants; in the South, it offers a haven for plants that would be defined as sun-lovers in regions with less intense sunlight. You can create high shade by removing the lower limbs

of trees. High shade depends largely on the type of tree: A mature oak, for example, might block light beneath its branches nearly completely; a fine-textured Japanese maple is more likely to create a pattern of filtered light.

Light Shade Similar to high shade in that a site with light shade receives bright light but no sustained, direct sunlight. The light may be reflected off a bright surface or filtered through branches. The branches' swaying and the sun's movement across the sky ensure that any sunbeam which does penetrate the canopy never focuses for long on a single spot.

Partial Shade More accurately described as partial sun. Areas of partial shade experience direct sunlight during part of the day. If this sunlight comes early or late in the day, its intensity will be far less than it would be in an area where the sun strikes around midday. In the South, shade at midday can be a plus even for plants grown in full sun elsewhere.

Dense Shade The perpetual shadow found underneath a thick tree canopy. Bulbs and wildflowers that grow and bloom in spring and retreat into dormancy in summer will flourish if the canopy consists of deciduous trees. Evergreens produce a far more challenging environment. Dense shade is often combined with dry shade.

Dry Shade Many deciduous shade trees, such as maples and beeches, as well as the most common evergreens, have roots that infiltrate soil right to the surface. During hot, dry weather, these roots quickly draw residual moisture from the soil. Plant such a site only with drought-tolerant plants.

The Unfamiliar Bulbs

Of course you know bulbs—what gardener doesn't? But how well do you really know them? Have you ever ventured beyond crocuses, daffodils, and tulips? Look a little further into the world of bulbs, and you'll find a host of intriguing alternatives. These unfamiliar bulbs offer the same convenience and reliability as the usual Dutch standbys. But they combine those virtues with all sorts of unexpected beauties and with a wide range of blooming seasons. Explore the unfamiliar, and you'll be planting bulbs into all sorts of new garden niches and enjoying a bulb display that lasts from spring through summer and on into fall.

Dwarf Narcissus

Hardy in zones 4 to 9, these miniatures offer classic daffodil blossoms on stems that commonly stand no more than 6 to 8 inches tall, and often less. Some of these dwarfs are nearly wild species, such as the petticoat daffodil *(Narcissus bulbocodium)* and *N. cyclamineus;* others are hybrids of garden origin. All are spring bloomers whose compact size makes them good flowers for small properties and for rock gardens, where a full-size daffodil would spoil the illusion of a miniature mountain landscape.

These miniatures are best appreciated close up. Martha has planted drifts of fragrant miniature narcissi such as 'Baby Moon' and 'Hawera' alongside a garden path, where passersby can appreciate the flowers' perfumes as well as their cheerful colors.

Dwarf narcissi require well-drained soil and will thrive in full sun, as well as in the shade of deciduous trees.

Muscari

These natives of the northeastern Mediterranean region are often called grape hyacinths because their diminutive flowers resemble tiny bunches of grapes. Commonly blue or purple (whites, pinks, and an occasional yellow may also be had), the flowers cluster around an upright stalk like a hyacinth's. Hardy in zones 3 to 8, they stand 6 to 12 inches tall, bearing one to three flowering stems per plant. Most muscari species reproduce by sprouting offsets (small bulbs) from the "mother" bulb and by self-sown seeds, so that as a group, these plants multiply rapidly. *Muscari armeniacum* and *M. neglectum,* in particular, can soon turn an early-spring bed or border or rock garden into a pool or cascade of flowers. The early-blooming *M. neglectum* is a great choice for naturalizing in shrub borders; it bears spires of white-rimmed deep-blue, almost-black, flowers topped by smaller, pale-blue flowers.

All varieties of muscari grow best in areas of full sun to light shade, and in a soil that is moist but well drained.

In her Connecticut garden, Martha pairs bulbs that bloom at the same time in complementary shapes and colors: low-growing cobalt blue grape hyacinths (Muscari armeniacum) and tall yellow-trumpeted daffodils (Narcissus). Tucking these spring-flowering bulbs among perennials such as Oriental poppies and shrubs such as tree peonies, both of which will flower later, gets the season off to an early start.

mixing bulbs

Allium

Some of these ornamental relatives of the onion verge on the bizarre, with flower stems up to 5 feet tall and flower heads like purple sunbursts that may measure a foot in diameter. In full bloom, they can look like a fleet of horticultural UFOs. Yet the genus *Allium* also includes plenty of subtler species, plants that stand barely 6 inches tall. Diversity is the alliums' hallmark. Purple is the most common hue, but blooms range from white through pale pink to deep rose, yellow, and clear blue, and the flower forms include wedge-shaped umbels as well as spheres and drooping tassels. No matter what the character of your garden, from spare, uncluttered elegance to cottage-style overabundance, there is an allium for you. Moreover, you'll find that its late-spring bloom neatly bridges the gap between the last late-flowering tulips and the earliest summer-flowering perennials.

Hardy in zones 3 to 8, alliums are for the most part sun-lovers, though a few species, such as white-and-green-flowered *Allium triquetrum,* tolerate light shade. Plant your alliums in sandy, well-drained soil loaded with compost and other organic matter, feed them at the beginning of the growing season with a slow-release bulb fertilizer, and give them at least $1/2$ inch of water every week from early spring through the end of bloom. Stop the irrigation after the flowers fade and the plants go dormant, with the straplike leaves dying back to the ground. Different allium species are naturally adapted to different climates and soils; find the ones adapted to your conditions, and they should return year after year.

Fritillaria

Eccentric charm is the best way to describe the flowers of the genus *Fritillaria*. In spring bloom they look like parasols of bells, striped, checked, or spotted in shades of smoky antique plum, mauve, gold, and near-black. When these flowers have a fragrance at all, it is skunky. Hardy in zones 3 to 9, the various species of fritillaries range in height from a couple of inches to 4 feet. Yet even the taller species tend to get lost in the competition of a crowded mixed border. *F. meleagris,* the foot-tall guinea-hen flower which bears checkered bells of purple or white, can hold its own amid small-scale wildflowers and grasses in a meadow garden. But most fritillaries are best showcased in the front of a bed, or in a rock garden. There they will find the full sun to light shade that they need and the moist but well-drained soil they prefer.

Gladiolus

Though their stiff, rather ungainly posture disqualifies gladioli from inclusion in her flower border, Martha couldn't imagine a summer without their blossoms in the cutting garden. For despite their heirloom status—gladioli were a Victorian favorite—these flowers come in a range of subtle yet sophisticated colors. The smaller-flowered miniatures, or pixiolas, are especially graceful.

Grow gladioli as annuals. Prepare the bed in fall to a depth of a foot and a half, working in well-rotted manure and a healthy dose of sand if the soil is heavy. Start the first plantings of gladiolus corms (bulbs) indoors in trays of potting mix set in a bright spot two to three weeks before transplanting into the garden, which should take place around the time of the last spring frost.

For a steady supply of cut flowers, make additional plantings every two weeks until early summer, gradually working your way from "early" varieties through "midseason" and "late." Depending on the variety, gladioli take 80 to 100 days to flower, and all want lots of sun and regular watering, but perfect drainage. Each stem of tall varieties must be staked, but wait until orientation of flower buds is obvious before tying in the stem below the lowest flower.

Dahlia

As a garden savior in the tough times of August through frost, the dahlia is unequaled. A full-size plant can easily fill a spot several feet across, solidly plugging a gap left by the demise of spring bloomers. Likewise, the flowers, which vary in form from pinwheels to pom-poms, and in size from less than 2 inches wide to 17-plus, can provide a whole garden's worth of bloom during that late summer lull when all else seems to be sulking.

Dahlia flowers swagger through the hot part of the color spectrum, ranging from white and pale yellow to vivid oranges and fire engine reds, although softer pinks and bronzes as well as cooler lavenders and purples are also available. The bicolors can look more tie-dyed than botanical. All in all, these are blossoms for an exuberant mood. And, as if the flowers were not enough, there are also dahlias with decorative foliage, such as the purple-bronze-leaved 'Bishop of Llandaff.'

Set out dahlias in the springtime, spacing them between 3 and 4 feet apart. Drive in a heavy stake beside each planting spot before putting in the tuber. Arrange the tubers horizontally between 4 and 6 inches below the surface, one to each hole and between 2 and 3 inches from a stake. A dose of 5-10-5 fertilizer and a thorough watering will get the dahlia going. Remove all but one of the emerging stems, and then tie the remaining stem to the stake. Pinching off the smaller side buds as they emerge from leaf bases along the stem channels the energy into fewer but larger blooms.

Dahlias flower through late summer, when many perennials have ceased to bloom. Although these bulbs may be grown as perennials in warm climates (zone 8 and south), they are treated as annuals in cold-winter areas. Northerners can dig up the bulbs (or tubers) in fall and store them for spring replanting.

lush summer bulbs

Shopping for Plants

Bargains are always welcome when you are shopping, but at the very least you want good value. Yet that is precisely what most people do not get when buying plants. Because they don't recognize the clues to quality, they settle for whatever the supplier has set out on the shelves of the local garden center, and if it meets their needs, that's as much good luck as anything else. Too often, what they bring home is a problem, which, if it doesn't die, only grows into a more serious problem.

It doesn't have to be that way. Arm yourself with the following checklist when you shop, and you can be confident of getting a vigorous specimen of a plant that fits your yard and your garden needs. You'll get the best price, and have a far more pleasant experience.

• **Wait for fall.** Delay shopping until after Labor Day: You'll find nurseries uncrowded and the nursery staff with plenty of time to answer questions. To avoid storing plants over the winter, nurseries commonly mark down the remaining stock by as much as 50 percent in fall. Besides, throughout the northern half of the United States, September is the best time to plant hardy evergreens, and late fall—October and November—is the best time to plant deciduous trees and shrubs. Fall is also an excellent season there for planting most kinds of perennial flowers. Where winters are mild, in the South and along the Pacific Coast, a late fall or early winter planting is ideal for virtually all kinds of garden plants except heat-loving annuals.

• **Don't bring problems home.** When shopping at a nursery, inspect plants closely for insect pests or their eggs before buying. Look at the undersides of leaves and at their bases along the stems, two spots where pests are likely to hide. Foliage stippled with lighter specks is also likely to be evidence of mite or insect infestation. Don't buy any infested plants; bringing them home can infest your whole garden.

• **Buy small.** Impatience encourages us to buy the largest tree and shrub specimens we can find, but to do so is usually an expensive mistake. Bigger specimens have larger root systems and so suffer more damage when dug for sale. Small specimens recover so much faster from transplanting that within a couple of years they commonly overtake the jumbo-size shrubs and trees that cost many times as much.

• **Ask about guarantees.** Mail-order nurseries offer a greater selection of plants than local garden centers, often at excellent prices. Before placing an order, however, call the customer-service number in the catalog and make sure that the firm has a policy of replacing without cost any plants that arrive at your address in poor condition. Such a policy is standard among the better mail-order nurseries.

• **Consider the season.** Beware of perennials, trees, and shrubs that are flowering or leafing out earlier than they should in your area. That's a sign that they came from a greenhouse or were grown in a milder region and shipped north. In either case, they may not prove hardy in your garden. Check their hardiness rating in a reliable reference before buying.

Top: A firm, evenly rounded root ball indicates that the nursery has carefully dug and wrapped a balled-and-burlapped (B & B) shrub or tree for transplanting. Seek out root balls secured with twine made from jute or other natural fibers; avoid nylon cord, which will not decompose in the ground. Above: Before purchasing a container-grown plant, ask to see it out of the pot. Beware of balls matted with white strands, a sign of a root-bound plant.

• **Examine the pot.** When shopping for container-grown plants, especially those of one-gallon size or larger, look for ribbed plastic pots. The ribs force emerging roots to grow back into the root ball, unlike smooth surfaced pots, which let roots circle the outside of the ball, thus encouraging the plant to become root-bound.

• **Remove the pot.** Before buying container-grown plants, ask the nurseryman to gently slip each one out of its pot. You should see crisp white root tips emerging from the soil, but the soil should not be encased in a sheet of encircling roots. Alternatively, examine the underside of the pot. Roots snaking out of the drainage holes in search of space and water are probably evidence that the plant is root-bound. Poke one finger between the pot wall and the soil to feel the root ball—it shouldn't feel like a thickened mass.

• **Check the roots.** Better nurseries keep container-grown plants from becoming root-bound by transplanting them into larger containers as they grow. You'll pay more for the larger plants, but at least you'll be getting healthy stock. Before you buy them, however, check that the plants are firmly rooted into the larger container. Why pay a premium for a one-gallon plant if it's really just a one-quart plant that was transplanted last week?

• **Buy green.** When purchasing annuals, particularly vegetables in cell packs, buy green. That is, buy the seedlings without fruits or flowers. The lanky tomato seedling in the 4-inch pot

that's already adorned with little fruits may seem like a sure thing, but in fact the premature harvest is evidence that the plant has been stressed. Such plants are also likely to be chlorotic, suffering from an iron deficiency that in green plants causes a yellowing or blanching of the leaves. Look for healthy, stout seedlings that are appropriate in size for their containers.

• **Eye the ball.** When shopping for B&B (balled and burlapped) trees or shrubs, pay close attention to the shape of the ball. Is it evenly formed or irregular? An irregular ball can mean a damaged root system; it may also be evidence that the ball was dropped. Be wary, too, of wire baskets. Though commonly used as reinforcement when balling and burlapping larger trees, with shrubs or trees whose trunk measures less than 3 inches in diameter, the wire basket is unnecessary. Unless, of course, the plant was grown in poor, sandy soil, or the root ball was damaged by careless digging.

• **Inspect for damage.** Before purchasing a tree or shrub, examine its skeleton. Broken branches or a split at the crotch (the spot where the trunk divides into the major branches) are evidence of careless handling and may be entry points for insects and diseases. Examine, too, the overall structure of branches and trunk. Is the tree or shrub well-formed and balanced? Does the crotch seem too tight or too low? If the plant starts with a weak or malformed skeleton, the adult will be weak and malformed, too.

Below: Tall seedlings, and those already adorned with flowers and fruits, may seem like a good buy. On the contrary, this precocious display usually marks stressed and stunted plants. A smaller yet sturdy, fully branched plant with buds is the better purchase. Bottom: Check nursery stock for damaged branches, which indicate mistreatment.

Ground Covers

Making a virtue of a necessity is the best kind of gardening, and ground covers certainly qualify as a necessity. They can free you from the slavery of mowing a lawn and reduce the need for weeding, watering, and even mulching. A flow of ground cover softens the hard edges of a house's corner, a patio, or a front stoop, and serves as camouflage for bulbs, whose unsightly foliage must stay in place after the flowers fade, or for leggy shrubs and perennials whose ankles look better clothed.

Ground covers are also experts at tying together loose ends. If you work drifts of one or, better yet, several interwoven ground covers into the landscape they can create a fabric that pulls together the disparate elements of trees, shrubs, and flowers. Of course, ground covers reinforce the landscape not just aesthetically but also physically, as they shore up erosion-prone banks and dunes. If handled skillfully, however, ground covers are more than an expedient. They transform the garden floor into a hardy mosaic, an attraction in its own right. To accomplish this, you must look beyond the simple sheet of green, the unblended (and predictable) expanse of pachysandra, ivy, or periwinkle *(Vinca minor)*. Instead, choose from the host of available species those that are suited to your garden's soil, light conditions, and climate. From these, in turn, select a handful that among them provide a variety of colors and textures. Pay particular attention to foliage, for that's what makes up the bulk of the garden picture, day in and day out.

Look for contrasts: small leaves to set against large ones, ferny leaves to partner with spiky or coarse. Colored or variegated leaves offer something extra, particularly for brightening shade. Flowering plants that need extensive deadheading—the removal of spent blossoms—are probably best avoided for such mass plantings. It's important, also, to select species of a height that fits the spot. Having settled on ferns, for instance, you next have to decide whether your design will better accommodate a six incher or a four footer.

Clever gardeners not only mix several principal plants but punctuate those with seasonal highlights like small bulbs or plants that color up in fall. Depending on what you plant, such a botanical crazy quilt can become a mountain meadow, a woodland floor, a Midwestern prairie, or even a lawn. But a lawn that requires little or no mowing and watering, a tough and informal turf of native buffalograss *(Buchloe dactyloides)* perhaps, or of grasslike sedges *(Carex* spp.), which, unlike conventional turf grasses, thrive in sun or shade, even where they must compete with tree roots.

Establishing a Ground Cover

Before planting, prepare the soil as you would for any other permanent garden. Strip away the turf (if any), skinning it off in sections with a sharp spade. Take extra care to dig out all roots of perennial weeds such as Bermuda grass and dandelions. To cleanse the soil of weed seeds, water the soil, wait a couple of weeks for seeds to germinate, and hoe out the resulting seedlings.

The number of plants needed to cover the area of prepared soil depends on the recommended spacing for the plants you have selected. Usually, the recommendation is expressed as a range: e.g., 6 to 10 inches. Selecting the closer spacing (6 inches rather than 10) obliges you to buy more plants, but it will help the ground cover knit together more quickly, and so reduce the threat of new invasion by weeds. Whatever spacing you select, cut a piece of wood to that length for use as a measuring stick.

If you are planting a slope with a grade steeper than 20 percent (that is, the slope rises or falls more than a foot over a distance of 5 feet), cover it with loosely woven, untreated burlap, which is sold in rolls of various widths and lengths as "lawn netting" or "erosion cloth." Drape the burlap loosely in

Gardening in Pots

Container gardeners consider every inch of the world fair game. Where others see obstinate surfaces—asphalt, brick, painted wood—these creative opportunists see occasions for more plants. Their windowsills are crowded with beloved green friends. Their patios are in full bloom. With their hanging baskets they hang a garden in midair.

The new fields for planting that container growing opens up are only one of its advantages. Planting in pots also lets us grow what our soil and climate say isn't wise: A hydrangea that won't turn pink in acidic terra firma can be made to do so, when potted up and dosed with limestone. A Ponderosa lemon tree thrives in a Minnesota garden all summer, so long as it and its tub are carried into a cool sunroom or greenhouse before the first frost.

Potted plantings give the garden remarkable flexibility. A perennial has faded, leaving an ugly gap in the border—so you drop in a pot in full bloom. Pot up a squad of boxwoods, and you have a team of portable exclamation points to push into a landscape in need of punctuation. On the night of a party, you can borrow them back to assemble around the terrace.

A single perfect specimen can make a striking statement, but for a lusher look, mix your plantings. At the container's heart, set a vertical centerpiece, some upright plant such as a canna, cordyline, or tibouchina, or anything that has been trained into a treelike "standard." Around the pot's outer edge arrange cascading plants such as ivy, sweet-potato vine, verbena, bidens, or petunia, so that their stems will spill out to soften the rim. Pack the remaining area with a mix of "fillers" such as coleus, pelargoniums, gomphrena, and salvias—plants that supply the color and body your pot needs.

The choice of plants for a potted garden is limited only by your imagination. Besides the usual annuals, flowering bulbs, perennials, ornamental grasses, shrubs, and small trees all adapt well to a life of containment. For the greatest interest, select containers with a variety of sizes and shapes. When you stage them as a group, emphasize the best pots by propping them up on inverted pots or bricks. If the result does not please you, it's easy to rearrange.

strips running up and down the slope, and pin these in place with 6-inch-long staples made from heavy-gauge wire. Overlap the strips of burlap 4 inches at the seams.

Buy ground covers as rooted cuttings in flats (trays containing up to 100 cuttings each) or in individual containers. Separate the cuttings in flats with a serrated kitchen knife, and arrange the plants on the prepared soil in staggered rows, using your measuring stick to keep the spacing uniform. If you cannot reach into the center of the bed without stepping onto the prepared soil, lay down a board or a scrap of plywood first to keep your feet from compressing the soil.

Plant flat-grown plants in holes just deep enough for their root masses and slightly wider. Plant larger, individual-container specimens as you would any container-grown plant (see page 44). On burlap-covered slopes, plant through slits cut into the cloth with a sharp pocketknife. On slopes with less than a 20 percent grade that haven't been burlapped, mound up a small berm around each plant's downhill side to catch runoff and prevent erosion.

Tuck in the plants with a layer of organic mulch, such as ground bark or pine needles, a couple of inches deep. Take care, though, to keep clear the area immediately surrounding each plant's crown; packing in the mulch too close may cause the plants to rot.

Water well, and irrigate regularly throughout the first growing season whenever the top inch of soil feels dry.

So long as the season is warm, anyone can "build" a tropical garden by combining a variety of plants in different-sized containers. Here, lofty yellow canna, low red-leaved coleus, and billowing blackfoot daisy (Melampodium leucanthum) can be left to knit together or be rearranged for new effects.

Containers make it possible
to garden where there is no true
ground to till. On this dock,
pots filled with a lightweight
soilless potting mix hold
abutilon, blackfoot daisies, can-
nas, coleus, ivy geraniums,
and sweet potato vine. For easy
maintenance, slow-release
fertilizer granules and water-
retaining polymer crystals
were added to the potting mix.

Tips for the Container Gardener

• Make sure that any container you use has several drainage holes in its bottom. Waterlogged soil is fatal to almost all potted plants.

• When plants outgrow a pot, move them to a pot just one size larger. "Overpotting"—setting a plant into a pot much larger than the root mass—will traumatize or even kill it.

• Pack your pots. Put in three times the plants you think they can hold. Then feed them generously.

• Consider using lightweight colored resin or fiberglass pots. They look like stone or terra cotta, but can help reduce the weight of container plantings, making them less of a load for decks and rooftops and easier to move on solid ground.

• To further reduce the weight of large containers, line their bottoms with 2 to 6 inches of Styrofoam packing peanuts before adding the potting mix and plants.

• For a lightweight potting medium with a perfect texture, use one of the ready-made soilless mixes sold by the bale at most garden centers. Improve it before use by working in time-release fertilizer at the rate recommended in the package directions.

• Container plantings dry out quickly, particularly in hot, sunny weather. Protect them from drought by adding water-absorbing polymer-gel crystals to the potting mix at the rate recommended on the product label. Soak the crystals first, so they are fully hydrated, and mix them into the potting mix in the container's lower half, before adding plants and more potting mix. The crystals, which release water slowly, significantly reduce the need for frequent watering.

• Damp pots set flat on a deck surface promote wood decay. Raise them on bricks to keep the deck surface dry.

• Feed potted plants with a liquid fertilizer every other week. Supplement several times a summer with a foliar feed of a diluted kelp-fish emulsion.

• Because hanging baskets' whole root ball is exposed to drying winds and sun, dehydration is more rapid. However, daily soakings leach out nutrients from the potting mix. Restore the mix with weekly feedings of a balanced all-purpose plant food.

• Rejuvenate root-bound plants, after overwintering them indoors, by root-pruning in early spring. Immerse container in water until bubbles stop rising from potting mix. Then slip plant out of container, and with a knife, slice edges off the root ball, rotating it and shaving each edge. Slice off matted bottom. In all, trim off one-eighth to one-third of old roots. If ball is still matted, slice into it from top to bottom three more times at even intervals around the circumference. Repot the plant so main stem is centered and crown (the point where roots and stem join) is an inch below rim, and refill with moistened potting mix enriched with time-release fertilizer. Don't place plant in direct sun until it has settled in.

Top: Houseplants can benefit from spending the summer outdoors, if they are given proper light. Leafy tree limbs, for example, temper the sun for glare-sensitive indoor plants and allow hanging pots to catch fresh air. Water plants regularly and feed every two weeks with a balanced fertilizer. Above: Potted African daisy (Arctotis) flourishes in full sun.

potting a plant

The way your plants are potted sets the tone for how they grow, so it's crucial to give them a good start. That means choosing both the potting mix and the pot with your particular plant in mind. The composition of potting mixes ranges from soilless to lean (containing a significant amount of coarse sand or grit, for cacti), from bulb-forcing mixes (with some grit) to general mixes (which comprise a balance of organic and inert matter). General mixes, of course, are blended to accommodate the widest range of plant needs. As for pots, remember that terra cotta is a porous material that allows for good air flow and drainage, but it can dry out; plastic pots tend to retain more water. And container size is key. A good rule of thumb is to select one that is about an inch longer than the root mass.

1 It all starts with the potting mix. First, the moisture content needs to be right. To check the moisture level, take a handful of mix, and make a ball with your fist. When you open your hand, the mix should hold together and crumble loosely when touched. If it falls apart right away it's too dry; if water drips out from the ball, it's too wet.

2 Pick a pot whose diameter is about an inch larger than the plant's root mass, and be sure it has a drainage hole. Cover the drainage hole in the bottom of the pot with a small shard of terra cotta to prevent the mix from washing out when the plant is watered. Then firm 1 inch of the mix into the bottom of the pot.

3 Center the plant in the pot so the roots can develop evenly all around. Place soil around the root mass, and gently firm it down with your fingers to eliminate air pockets. The plant's crown should be even with the soil level and about 1 inch below the pot's rim. This space will work like a water well when you water your plants and will prevent soil from washing out over the rim.

4 Water your plant with a watering can or by bottom watering. In the case of bottom watering, place the potted plant in a tub or sink. Fill it with water halfway up the side of the pot. Water will wick up into the mix through the drainage hole in the pot's bottom. Check the soil surface for moisture. It should not take more than half an hour to saturate the mix. Remove the pot from its bath, and allow excess water to drain out the bottom.

Troughs

British gardeners began recycling old stone livestock troughs more than a century ago, turning these outsized containers into miniature alpine landscapes. The originals are costly antiques today, but you can easily make your own trough, a lightweight version that nevertheless looks as if it has been chipped from stone, with a simple mold and less than twenty dollars' worth of concrete, peat moss, and horticultural perlite. By including peat moss in the mix, you make the walls of your creation an inviting habitat for mosses, algae, and lichens. Except in arid climates, these botanical colonists will soon spread across your handiwork, giving the concrete a patina of antiquity by the end of its first season outdoors.

Because these homemade troughs are porous, they are especially hospitable to plants that require exceptionally good drainage. Alpine plants flourish in them, and by intermingling the plants with stones and a gravel mulch, you can turn your trough into a Swiss mountaintop. Using succulents and cacti, by contrast, you can create a desertscape; with creeping thyme and a compact Japanese maple or miniature elm, you have a woodland. A trough also makes an unusual and handsome raised bed for an herb garden or for small vegetables such as salad greens.

Whatever you decide to plant in the troughs you construct, don't make just one. Casting bottomless risers to place under the troughs adds a new design dimension. Rather than placing troughs simply in a row, these "blocks" allow a wall of planters to be built up from the ground. By raising the planters, you'll encourage cascading plants that can soften the edges of the craggy planters. Be creative; try different shapes. Circular or rectangular, octagonal or oval, any shape is worth trying and will add a surprising twist to your planters.

Ideal homes for alpine and miniature plants, troughs can be cast in an array of shapes and arranged in all sorts of configurations. In this multilevel trough garden, the containers are stacked irregularly to create a sculptural "landscape" that gives every plant the best possible orientation for sunlight and ventilation. Spreading plants have walls to spill over, and mosses have porous surfaces to grasp.

casting a garden trough

Materials:

2 cardboard boxes, one slightly smaller than the other

4 four-inch-long pieces of ³/₄-inch wooden dowel

1 roll of 36-inch-wide ³/₄-inch-mesh chicken wire

1 eighty-pound bag of Portland cement

1 large bag of horticultural perlite

1 small (2.2 cubic feet) bale of sphagnum peat

1 Gather materials. One of the two cardboard boxes you use should be slightly smaller than the other: The space between the two will determine the thickness of the trough's walls. You will also need dowels, chicken wire, and Portland cement, which will give the trough a weathered, almost aged-stone look. Plan to take about 2 hours to assemble the mold and pour the cement.

2 In a tub or wheelbarrow, mix 3 parts (by volume) horticultural perlite with three parts sphagnum peat and two parts Portland cement. Be sure to wear a mask while mixing to avoid inhaling hazardous cement dust.

3 Wearing waterproof gloves to protect your hands, work enough water into your perlite-peat-cement mix to give it the consistency of moist cottage cheese. The mix will appear darker at this stage than it will when it dries.

4 Place the larger cardboard box on a drop cloth with its opening facing up. Any tape, seams, or gouges in the cardboard will appear as impressions on the finished trough, so be sure that the inside surface of the box is to your liking (keeping in mind that some rough textures are desirable). To make the bottom of the trough, pour in a 1-inch layer of the cement mix. Cut ³/₄-inch mesh chicken wire to the same shape as the box, but 1 inch smaller on all sides. Place it on top of the first layer of wet cement mix for reinforcement. Then top this with another 1-inch layer of cement. Lightly smooth the surface to even it off.

These garden troughs are especially well suited to people who aren't perfectionists in the garden. Irregular shapes and rough edges only enhance the natural-looking qualities that make these troughs so desirable. Once you understand the basics of making garden troughs, you can experiment with myriad variations to create striking designs. Plastic wastebaskets and take-out soup containers make great molds, large and small. Remember, though, that removing the finished trough requires the destruction of the mold.

5 Push the dowel pieces through the center of the cement mix lining the box's bottom, spacing them 3 to 4 inches apart. These will be removed later to make drainage holes in the bottom of the finished trough.

6 Fold the flaps of the smaller box inward, and tape them flush against the sides. Place that box upside down on the cement inside the larger box. Center a layer of chicken wire in the space between the sides of the two boxes. The top of the wire mesh should rest 1 inch lower than the boxes' upper edges, so that metal won't poke out of the walls of the finished trough.

7 Using a mason's trowel, fill the mold with cement mix. As the walls of the trough rise, periodically push a wide stick into the mix to tamp it down and eliminate any air pockets. If you wish to give the trough a decorative touch, push seashells, stones, colored glass, pieces of ceramic, or other objects down the interior of the larger box as you fill the mold. Be careful not to put in so many items that the walls end up with more decoration than concrete.

8 When the mold is filled and the wire reinforcement hidden, smooth the top edges of the cement with a trowel. Cover the mold with a plastic sheet to keep the cement moist while it sets. Let the trough cure for up to 5 days, but no less than 24 hours. Once the cement is set, rip out the inner box, pull out the dowels, and tear away the outer cardboard. Apart from developing an occasional crack or pit, which enhances its aged look, the trough can last for years. Should repair become necessary, apply a patch of moistened perlite-peat-cement mix with the mason's trowel.

Shrubs, Trees, and Lawn

Shrubs may well be the closest thing to a no-maintenance plant this side of the petrified forest. Plant them, feed them occasionally, prune them (maybe) once a year—otherwise, just enjoy. The right tree in the right place is another solid investment. Throughout most of the growing season, both shrubs and trees define a living framework sturdy enough to keep a vigorous collection of perennials and annuals from degenerating into an unruly menagerie. Then, in winter, the same shrubs and trees stand out as the garden's most enduring, and endearing, structure. • Controversy, however, surrounds another element of garden design: the lawn. For more than a century, Americans have loved the way mowed turf sets off the garden's varied colors, shapes, and textures. Recently, that same lawn has come under fire as an environmental hazard. There's truth in both points of view, but also a broad middle ground where we can garden responsibly and happily.

*Sheared into living walls, a row of shrubs or trees can divide a garden into "rooms," act as privacy screens, or conceal unsightly views. Here, a hedge of olive trees (*Olea europaea*) echoes the geometry of house and paving while its foliage softens the expanse of stucco and brick. A white potato vine (*Solanum jasminoides*) trained onto a lattice frame creates another "wall."*

Hardworking Shrubs

These many-stemmed woody plants have been described as the workhorses of the garden, and that's true, as far as it goes. Shrubs do play a disproportionate role in making the garden work. They sprawl across beds as ground covers and stand shoulder to shoulder in screens and hedges to enclose planting areas, divide one outdoor room from the next, and conceal eyesores. Shrubs furnish shade and shelter from the wind to sensitive perennials planted at their feet, stabilize slopes with their roots, fill vases with cut flowers and foliage, and provide cover and berries to wildlife.

Still, in appreciating all the vital services that shrubs can provide, it can be easy to overlook their aesthetic qualities. Few other garden plants are so lovely, and lovely in so many different ways. There are the perfumes of the flowers, their colors, and the colors of the leaves and twigs. Shrubs offer an endless variety of profiles and silhouettes, from creeping to columnar, and a presence that, depending on the species, can be reassuringly massive or tantalizingly diaphanous. And for the gardener with a taste for architectural formality, many shrubs may be clipped or sheared into precise, geometric shapes. Especially in wintertime, when so many other garden plants have died or retreated underground, shrubs play a starring role in our landscapes. Struggling into boots, coat, and gloves will seem a small price to pay for a view of Harry Lauder's walking stick (*Corylus avellana* 'Contorta') and the fantastic tracery that shrub's curled and twisted twigs make against the new-fallen snow.

Clipped hedges can be used like pedestals, to set off the sculptural shapes and textures of other shrubs and trees' natural growth patterns. Here, a low, well-groomed yew (Taxus) *hedge contrasts with the rich mix of unclipped conifers and deciduous trees that rise and spread above it: From left, cypress* (Chamaecyparis), *juniper* (Juniperus), *and Japanese maple* (Acer palmatum).

a mix of textures

Four-Season Shrubs

When choosing garden shrubs, we tend to focus on the flowers. That's not surprising, but it is shortsighted. For, spectacular as the blossoms may be, most of them are a passing pleasure. With a few exceptions, any given shrub blooms no more than three to four weeks each year; for the remaining forty-eight-plus weeks, the shrub's other attributes (those we overlooked when choosing the plant) determine its impact on the landscape. That's why, when selecting shrubs, you should always take the four-season perspective.

You will discover that there's a whole class of harder-working shrubs, four-season performers that have something to offer every day of the year. Most of the four-season shrubs have flowers we love, and yet they also bear colorful fruits and handsome foliage.

But it's when winter puts an end to those obvious attractions that these shrubs' subtler charms emerge: the colorful stems, the bicolor or peeling bark, the prominent winter buds, the unusual textures or patterns of the branches, the harmony of the shrubs' overall form. Any of these attributes can make a plant special, but in combination they make a shrub a four-season winner. Here are some standouts:

Amelanchier Light, airy, and graceful, amelanchiers—also known as serviceberries or shadbushes—flash pure white, fleecy flowers along the woodland's edge every spring. But flowers are only one of the attractions of these 15- to 20-foot-tall shrubs.

The new leaves that emerge with or just after the blossoms are reddish-bronze, and they mature to a cool blue-green. The clusters of fruit quickly turn red, then ripen to a deep blue-black. Besides attracting birds, this fruit makes pies and preserves that rival the best of blueberries.

Fall brings wonderful yellowish-orange to red foliage, and in winter the structure of the fine branches and the smooth, gray bark provides a perfect scaffold for snow.

There are many fine amelanchiers, but one of the best is *Amelanchier* x *grandiflora* 'Autumn Brilliance,' a cultivar whose glowing red fall foliage often hangs on late into the season. Other fail-safe options are the *Amelanchier* x *grandiflora* cultivars 'Cole's Select,' which also sports outstandingly rich, red fall color, and 'Robin Hill,' whose pink buds fade to white as the flowers open.

Amelanchiers are not recommended for the warmer areas of the Southwest or the Pacific coast's more humid areas; elsewhere, however, these shrubs are extraordinarily reliable.

Amelanchier

*Apple serviceberry (*Amelanchier *x* grandiflora*), shown in its full silhouette, below left, is one of the approximately twenty-five species in this genus of deciduous shrubs and trees. All are prized for their pale spring blossoms, tasty fruits, and colorful fall foliage.*

Cornus and Salix Though we think of willows *(Salix)* and dogwoods *(Cornus)* as trees, both genera include a good number of shrubby species. Many offer handsome foliage. *Salix integra* 'Itakuro Nishiki,' for example, a relatively compact 5-foot-tall shrub, bears leaves variegated with pink, cream, and green. And the willow's early spring blossoms, the velvety "pussies," provide one of the most sensually satisfying textures in the plant world. But the outstanding attraction of the shrubby willows and dogwoods is undoubtedly their vividly colored stems, which burn brightest in the otherwise bleak landscape of winter.

The most brilliant *Salix* is the coral bark willow, *Salix alba* 'Britzensis,' whose tan, rose, and apricot stems truly glow. *Cornus stolonifera,* the red osier, is the dogwood star. Its cultivar 'Cardinal' has stems that are red in late fall and then turn pink in winter and chartreuse in spring, while 'Flaviramea' has yellow stems and 'Silver and Gold' offers both yellow stems in winter and creamy-edged variegated leaves in summer. With all of these shrubs, the new twigs are the most brilliant; to keep them at peak color, cut the shrubs back to the ground every second or third spring.

Ilex Don't wait for Christmas to celebrate with hollies *(Ilex),* which include many of the finest broad-leaved evergreens. Particularly elegant are the blue hollies *(Ilex x meserveae),* whose leaves are a lustrous blue green, and whose white flowers are followed by loads of shiny red fruits—if you provide your female specimens with a male consort. 'Blue Girl' forms a pyramidal shrub 8 to 10 feet tall; 'Blue Princess' reaches a height of 15 feet and a width of 10 feet; 'Blue Prince' (the berryless but necessary male) is bushy, growing to 8 to 12 feet. All are widely adapted to Northern regions.

For a similar effect in the Southern states (including Florida), rely on *Ilex cornuta* 'Burfordii' (10 to 15 feet tall), *I. cornuta* 'Dwarf Burford' (about 5 feet), and the very heavily fruiting yaupon holly *I. vomitoria* 'Pride of Houston.' *I. cornuta* 'D'or' started as a sport, a mutation that appeared as a single branch on a bush of *I. cornuta* 'Burfordii.' In most respects, this sport is similar to its parent, with dark, almost black-green, very glossy leaves and a densely rounded shape, but 'D'or' offers one striking contrast: bright golden berries instead of the standard scarlet.

Clockwise from top left: The flower of Ilex cornuta; *foliage and berries of* I. x meserveae 'Blue Girl'; *a leaf of* I. x meserveae 'Blue Princess'; *the shape of a mature* I. cornuta 'Burfordii.'

Vaccinium Blueberries belong in your garden, not just on your cereal. Both the lowbush blueberry, *Vaccinium angustifolium,* which tops out at a height of less than 2 feet, and the highbush, *V. corymbosum,* which grows 6 to 12 feet tall, combine delicate whitish-pink flowers, lustrous fine-textured, dark-green summer foliage, delicious deep-blue berries, orange-red fall foliage, and yellow-green to reddish winter twigs. They contribute in every season, though the early-summer berry harvest is what attracts flocks of birds and children.

Blueberries need acid soil—highbush will grow well even in Florida if the soil pH is right. Outstanding highbush cultivars include 'Northland,' 'Northblue,' and 'Elliott'; 'Northsky' is a lowbush cultivar with particularly tasty fruits. In the Pacific Northwest, the related lingonberry, *V. vitis-idaea,* provides a native alternative; its cultivar 'Koralle' forms a low, evergreen ground cover with deep-red fruit and mahogany winter foliage. Across the Southeast and Southwest, *V. arboreum,* farkleberry, is a welcome large drought- and heat-tolerant, spreading shrub with white flowers, leathery dark-green leaves, and peeling bark that ranges from gray brown through orange and reddish brown. Its black fruits are decorative but inedible.

Viburnum The doublefile viburnum, *Viburnum plicatum* f. *tomentosum,* ranks near the top of any list of must-have shrubs. The doublefiles are large shrubs whose branches reach out in a distinctive pattern of horizontal tiers, which in springtime are covered with 6-inch disks of creamy to white flowers that perch atop the branches as if just resting. The fruits, a carmine red that gradually changes to black, are a magnet for birds. In fall, the green leaves blush to a mahogany-wine hue.

'Mariesii' is a popular cultivar that reaches a height of almost 12 feet; 'Shasta' grows about 6 feet high and 10 to 12 feet wide. Compact 'Summer Snowflake' tops out at just 4 to 6 feet; it blooms continually throughout the summer. Doublefile viburnums flourish everywhere in zones 5 through 8, except in southern Florida and the Southwest, where *V. suspensum* is a better choice. A large evergreen shrub, this bears fragrant, pale-pink flowers followed by red berries that mature to black. North of zone 5, try *V.* x *rhytidophylloides* 'Allegheny,' a dense shrub no more than 8 feet tall, which produces white flowers and fruits that change from yellow to red to black, often bearing all three colors at once.

Viburnum

Clockwise from bottom left: The characteristic
growth pattern of Viburnum rufidulum; a
fall leaf of V. plicatum f. tomentosum; a flower
of V. shasta; fruits of V. x rhytidophylloides.

Easy Roses

Other Options While filling out your shrubbery schedule, don't forget the witchhazels *(Hamamelis)* and their cousins, *Fothergilla major* and *F. gardenii.* Their fragrant flowers bracket the seasons: Common witchhazel, *H. virginiana,* blooms in mid- to late fall, and Chinese witchhazel, *H. mollis,* as early as February; both fothergillas are spring bloomers. All of the above have interesting leaves with great fall color.

A four-season star among rhododendrons is *Rhododendron yakushimanum.* This gracefully mounded shrub bears large, spectacular flowers set off by dark-green evergreen leaves that are light gray-brown and woolly on the undersides. Superior *R. yakushimanum* cultivars include 'Yaku Angel,' 'Yaku Prince,' and 'Yaku Queen.'

Finally, it may take some hunting to locate a specimen of *Heptacodium miconioides,* the seven-son flower from China, but it's worth the search. A relatively new arrival in our gardens, this shrub thrives throughout most of the United States. After clothing itself with dark-green leaves in early spring, it sprouts red flower buds that open in late summer into fragrant yellowish-white flowers that are borne seven to a stem. As the petals drop, the remnants of the flowers turn a reddish purple. Round out the year in wintertime by enjoying the *Heptacodium's* light-tan, papery exfoliating (peeling) bark.

There's no question about the identity of America's favorite flower. Roses are what we send our sweetheart on Valentine's Day, what we wear on our lapel and carry in the bouquet when we marry, and what we bring home to patch up an argument. Still, much as we love roses, fewer and fewer of us grow them.

We keep roses out of our gardens because we believe that they are fussy shrubs requiring constant catering. That's what they are, too—if you grow the common run of hybrid tea and floribunda roses, the roses you find lined up in boxes and pots every spring at the garden center. These two breeds of roses are like thoroughbred horses: capable of phenomenal performance, but delicate.

If, however, you expand your definition of roses, and explore the many other breeds, old and new, currently available at specialty mail-order rose nurseries, you'll find plants that produce the flowers you want but require no more care than a lilac or an azalea. What's more, you'll find that these easy roses are admirable shrubs even when not in bloom. Their healthy handsome foliage and attractive, balanced branching structure make them easy to integrate with the rest of your landscape. Instead of isolating these shrubs in a "roses only" rose garden, you'll be using them all over.

Choosing the Right Roses

Roses are regional plants—each breed or "class" prefers a certain climate and soil. Martha, for instance, has found gallica roses, a breed perfected in nineteenth-century France, to be winter hardy and disease resistant in both her New York and Connecticut gardens. These compact shrubs bloom only once a year, in early summer, but they bear flowers of antique elegance, including many that are streaked and marbled with contrasting colors and others of a velvety wine-purple seen in no other rose. Gallicas are easy to grow throughout the Northeast and Midwest, but if you garden in the Southeast, you'll find they have difficulty coping with your summer heat. You will have far greater success with tea roses (ancestors of the modern hybrid teas) or China roses, two other antique classes that bloom and rebloom repeatedly throughout the growing season.

Glossary of Easy Roses, by Class
Modern Roses

Canadian Explorer Robust, disease-resistant, cold- and wind-proof shrubs from the Canadian Ministry of Agriculture's experiment station in Ottawa. Hardy to zone 3 or even 2, a safe choice for all northern regions. 'Henry Hudson' is white, 'Jens Munk' pink, 'Champlain' white. 'Henry Kelsey' is a red climbing rose, 'William Baffin' a deep pink climber.

Hybrid Tea The classic florist's roses; bloom repeatedly through warm weather. Best adapted to Southwest; grow disease-resistant cultivars such as 'Folklore' (orange-pink), 'Helen Traubel' (apricot), 'Mister Lincoln' (red), and 'Pascali' (white).

'William Baffin,' a rose in the Canadian Explorer class, is one of the hardiest, most disease-resistant modern climbers. Like all climbers, which naturally put out long, supple canes, this repeat-bloomer shows to best advantage when trained onto a fence or trellis.

Floribunda Bloom repeatedly, bearing clusters of cupped or hybrid-tea-type flowers. Cold hardier than hybrid teas (typically to zone 5, some cultivars to zone 4). Best in arid Western climates. Disease-resistant cultivars include 'Europeana' (red), 'Gene Boerner' (pink), 'Iceberg' (white), and 'Sun Flare' (yellow).

Griffith Buck Repeat blooming, with broad, bright color range and flower forms of hybrid teas, but disease resistant and cold tolerant. Bred for Midwest; good also in Northeast, Northwest, and Rocky Mountain West.

Hybrid Musk Repeat-blooming shrubs with small flowers borne in sprays. Hardy to zones 4 or 5, but also excellent in Southeast and Southwest. Disease-resistant cultivars include 'Cornelia' (apricot pink), 'Ballerina' (rose pink, white at center), and 'Lavender Lassie' (lavender pink).

Meidiland Bred specifically for use as landscape shrubs, these are exceptionally disease-resistant and naturally compact reblooming roses that need little pruning. Meidilands thrive in zones 4 through 9. 'Carefree Wonder' is pink, 'Scarlet Meidiland' red, 'White Meidiland' white.

Rugosa Repeated, fragrant bloom, huge decorative fruits, colorful fall foliage. Exceptionally disease- and drought resistant. Hardy to zone 2; rugosas do not thrive in zones 8 and 9.

Roses old and new (left, top to bottom): The hybrid tea 'Dainty Bess'; the floribunda 'Lavender Pinocchio'; the hybrid musk 'Penelope'; and the gallica 'Charles de Mills.'

Heirloom Roses

Alba, Gallica, and Damask Cold-hardy, long-lived shrubs that generally bloom once in early summer (some damask roses rebloom in fall). Very fragrant flowers in delicate shades of white, pink, and red—no yellows or oranges. Albas form graceful, mounded shrubs; gallicas are more compact. Both are excellent for the Northeast, Northwest, and Midwest. Damasks perform especially well in dry Western climates.

China, Noisette, Tea Reblooming; thrive in warm climates, dry or humid. Chinas have numerous small flowers in reds, pinks, white, and occasionally yellow; noisettes are climbers or sprawling shrubs that bear sprays of perfumed blossoms in whites, pinks, golds, and apricot; teas are shrubs or climbers with oversize, heavy blossoms in white, pink, red, and yellow.

Caring for Easy Roses

Reblooming types should get full sun for at least half of each day; the once-blooming old-fashioned roses and the species roses thrive in sun or bright shade. Good air circulation is essential; don't crowd roses.

Remove any winter-killed branches in spring, and feed then, too: Irrigate soil around roses with a mixture of fish emulsion and kelp extract. Feed again with the same mixture as the first flush of flowers opens, and once more in fall with just the kelp extract, to enhance winter hardiness. If your soil is poor in organic matter or prone to drying out, mulch around roses with a couple of inches of compost in spring and fall.

pruning roses

1 Inspect plants carefully in springtime. The new growth reveals which canes and branches made it through the winter alive. Remove any dead canes by cutting them off at the base. Branches partially killed by winter weather should be cut back to a spot just above a vigorously growing bud.

2 At this time it is also good to prune off any broken canes or branches on the rose bush. Also prune any that have been injured by grazing rabbits or deer. Canes should be cut back to a healthy side branch or, in the case of a heavily damaged cane, cut off right at the base.

3 Check the remaining branches closely. Blotches of matte brown, perhaps edged with purple, spreading over the greenish bark, are symptoms of canker, a disease that may be caused by any of several fungi. New shoots may be emerging around and above the cankers, but these will die as the disease spreads and girdles the stem. Prune off all such diseased wood, making your cuts well below the lowermost cankers. Dispose of infected debris, but do not add it to your compost bin.

4 Also cut off at their base any weak and spindly canes, and canes or branches that are growing back through the center of the bush. Air cannot circulate through a bush congested with ingrown branches, and this fosters fungal diseases such as blackspot. Use a lopper to cut through thick canes.

5 For especially thick or hard old wood, cut with a pruning saw. All bush-type roses should have remaining canes shortened by a half to a third to promote compact, sturdy growth; the best time for this varies with the type of rose. Because repeat-flowering "everblooming" roses, such as hybrid teas and floribundas, bloom most heavily on new shoots, cane-shortening should be carried out in early spring when deadwood is removed. Old-fashioned roses that bloom once a year bear flowers only on branches at least a year old. Shortening their canes in early spring removes much of the branches that would bear flowers in succeeding months. So wait until right after they bloom to shorten canes of once-bloomers.

6 Climbing roses, even reblooming modern types such as climbing hybrid teas, also bear the bulk of their flowers in an early summer flush. Wait until this subsides before shortening all horizontal side branches by a half to a third. Leave the main skeleton of upright canes intact, unless renewing a neglected specimen (see page 116).

7 Besides keeping your pruning shears clean and sharp, you should disinfect them to prevent the spread of diseases and pathogens from one rose plant to the next. Both before and after pruning, dip the blades of the pruners into isopropyl alcohol.

Age first brings a handsome maturity to shrubs, but then, eventually, senility. Stems thicken, growing less flexible and gradually losing vigor, so that they bear fewer flowers and fruits. In most cases, it's easy to reverse this decline by forcing the shrub to replace its failing stems and branches with new growth. Be careful, however, in attempting to renew dwarf conifers, since many needled evergreens generate new growth from the tips of existing branches.

1. Check the chart on page 119 to determine whether a shrub sprouts suckers, or new shoots, from the base of stems or from the roots. If not, cut back overage stems to a side branch to force out new growth.

2. Some fast-growing suckering shrubs, such as shrubby dogwoods and willows, respond well to a drastic approach: In early spring, all old stems are cut back to ground level.

3. Other, slower-growing suckering shrubs, such as lilacs and spireas, respond better to a gradual treatment whereby one-third of the old stems are removed each year for three years in a row. Cut older stems to the ground after selecting a sucker to keep as its replacement. Thin additional suckers to prevent congestion. If a shrub

has no existing suckers, fertilize and prune stems back to a side branch to encourage suckering; begin renewal the following year.

4. With older climbing roses, remove one old cane each year, in early summer right after the first flush of flowers fades. Tie in a flexible young cane as its replacement.

Shrub Pruning

Maybe it's the finality of this process—you amputate a branch or limb, and there's no reattaching it, even if you decide that you've made a mistake. But whatever the reason, taking up the pruning shears or saw paralyzes even many veteran gardeners.

Two thoughts, though, should take much of the anxiety out of pruning: First, recognize that pruning is inevitable. If you don't make the cuts, it will be a storm that carries away a weak branch or shortens the trunk that has grown too long. Leave deadwood on a shrub, and wood-decaying fungi will take it off. Fail to thin the branches of a congested shrub, and disease will do it for you. If you don't prune, these natural agents surely will, but they will also remove branches in ways that traumatize or kill the plant.

The second thing to keep in mind about pruning is that it's easy to do right. Before you set to work on any shrub, make sure you understand the growth patterns of that particular species. Understand the shape—conical, mounded, creeping, etc.—that the shrub naturally adopts, and try to enhance it with your cuts. Understand, too, how the shrub grows, whether new growth springs from the tips of its branches or from the base of the trunk, and whether it is new twigs or old that will produce the flowers, fruits, and colorful bark you want. Understand these things, and each shrub will tell you how to prune it.

Maintenance Pruning

To be most effective, shrub pruning must be a regular feature of your gardening schedule. A regular program of minor cuts—maintenance pruning—allows you to direct the growth of these plants into a healthy pattern. By giving each shrub a few minutes of attention annually, you can usually forestall the need for major, sometimes tragic, surgery down the road. In this way, you'll save yourself a great deal of work while protecting your shrubs against the traumas of drastic cuts and large wounds.

Timing is important. Pruning in late winter or early spring, right before a shrub emerges from dormancy, generally causes the least trauma to the plant. Northern gardeners, though, usually wait for new growth to appear so that they can identify winter-killed branches. As with roses (see page 115) the right pruning schedule can also enhance flowering. To promote the best bloom, it's usually wise to prune spring-blooming shrubs after they flower, and summer- and fall-blooming shrubs as they emerge from dormancy. There are exceptions, so be sure to check recommendations for specific shrubs in the pruning chart on page 119.

Remove the three Ds. Dead, damaged, and diseased branches—it's important to remove them all.

Trim crossing branches. Cut out one of any pair of crossing branches—branches that overlap and rub against one another; the wounds this friction causes offer an entry for diseases and pests.

Relieve crowding. Cut off at the base any branches that are growing back into the center of the bush. These are the botanical equivalents of ingrown toenails; as the wind tosses them, they injure the canes and branches around them. They also create congestion, providing a hiding place for insect pests and a perfect nursery for fungal diseases.

Prune young shrubs. While the shrub is young, prune it to create an armature of well-spaced, spreading branches. Visualize the shape that a particular species of shrub characteristically adopts; if you don't know the shape, ask your nurseryman. Select the branches on the young shrub that promise to fit that profile nicely as they grow, and remove at the base any other branches that crowd or compete with your selections. After the first or second pruning session, the structure should be well established, and this part of the pruning process should require no more than a few snips every year.

Remove suckers. Some types of shrubs, including most roses, commonly sprout new shoots, or "suckers," from the point where the stems join the roots, or from the roots themselves. Suckers are always undesirable on grafted plants—a group that includes most roses—if they emerge from below the point where the top growth joins the rootstock. Remove such suckers at the base. Newly emerged suckers may simply be wrenched off the crown; to remove those sprouting from the

roots, excavate to expose where the sucker emerges from the roots, cut it off there, and then replace the soil. With ungrafted plants, suckers can be used to renew declining specimens (see "Renewing Neglected Shrubs," opposite), but if allowed to multiply unchecked they soon turn a shrub into a thicket. Therefore, remove most of the suckers as they appear, leaving only those desired as the source of a new trunk or stem.

Above right: When a branch is broken, cut it cleanly to remove the damaged segment. Center right: Use a pruning saw to cut off crowded stems or trunks that are too thick for shears to handle. Bottom right: Take out branches that grow into the center of the shrub.

At the garden of Mabel Harkness in Geneva, New York, the hybrid lilac Syringa chinensis 'Sangeana' puts on a grand show. To maintain the shape of a specimen like this, prune it after the blossoms have faded.

shrub pruning guide

Shrub	Suckers?	When to Prune	Notes
Azalea (Rhododendron)	After hard pruning.	Immediately after flowering.	Rarely needs pruning.
Boxwood (Buxus species)	Sprouts from branches cut back to bare wood.	Spring to midsummer in cold climates; year-round in mild.	Remove only damaged branches. May be sheared as formal hedge.
Butterfly bush (Buddleia davidii)	Yes.	Any time from late fall to early spring.	Cut back all stems to within a few inches of the ground.
Camellia (Camellia spp.)	Sprouts from trunks cut to bare wood.	After flowering.	Requires little pruning. To rejuvenate, cut back or remove old trunks.
Cotoneaster (Cotoneaster spp.)	Rarely.	Late winter or early spring just before growth begins.	Little pruning needed; to restrain growth, prune back stems to side branch.
Dogwood (Cornus spp.)	Yes.	Late winter for colorful twig types; after bloom for flowering trees.	Colored-twig species: Cut back stumps in late winter. Trees: little or no pruning.
Forsythia (Forsythia spp.)	Vigorously; branch tips may sucker if touching ground.	Immediately after flowering.	Remove older stems, cutting back to ground; remove excess suckers.
Holly (Ilex spp.)	Most sucker sparingly in response to hard pruning.	Spring; summer pruning reduces berry production.	Pruning rarely needed. Remove $1/3$ of stems annually, 3 years in a row.
Juniper (Juniperus spp.)	Sprouts from branches cut back to bare wood.	Spring, before new growth begins; shear hedge whenever needed.	Avoid hard pruning; it destroys junipers' naturally graceful shapes.
Lilac, common (Syringa vulgaris)	Yes; thin regularly.	Immediately after flowering.	Cut stems to spur branching. Remove $1/3$ of old stems annually, 3 years in a row.
Nandina (Nandina domestica)	Suckers from the roots.	Spring, before new growth begins.	Remove old stems periodically.
Pieris (Pieris spp.)	Sprouts from branches and trunks cut to bare wood.	After flowering.	Needs little pruning. Renew by cutting back trunks over 2 to 3 years.
Japanese barberry (Berberis thunbergii)	Sprouts from branches cut to bare wood.	Spring or early to midsummer; avoid late hard pruning.	Tolerates shearing; good for a hedge.
Rhododendron	Sprouts from branches and trunks cut to bare wood.	After flowering for maintenance.	To renew, remove $1/3$ of old stems.
Spirea (Spiraea spp.)	Most sucker readily.	S. x bumalda, S. japonica: early spring; S. x vanhouttei, S. thunbergii: right after bloom.	Each year cut some of oldest stems at ground level.
Viburnum (Viburnum spp.)	Yes.	Early spring (V. x burkwoodii, V. dentatum, V. opulus, V. setigerum, V. trilobum after bloom).	Occasional removal of older, failing stems encourages new growth.
Weigela (Weigela florida)	Yes.	After flowering.	Remove oldest stems annually.
Yew (Taxus spp.)	Sprouts from branches cut back to bare wood.	Shear in spring or early summer; prune hard only in early spring.	Remove $1/3$ of old stems annually, 3 years in a row.

Trees in Winter

Pull on your hat and gloves, wrap on the muffler—winter's here, and that makes it time for a walk in the nearest arboretum. For this is the season when trees shed their warm-weather cladding and expose their true character. Trees, of course, are always the backbone of the garden, its major presence, but never more so than now. With the flowers dead or dormant and the lawn the color of baled hay, the woody plants—and trees above all—are what give the garden structure and interest. Besides, when the trees are stripped of foliage, you can really see the pattern of their branches, the color and texture of their bark; you can see their profiles silhouetted against the winter sky and better choose the ones that will enhance your garden all year round.

The buttressed base of a copper beech, for example, stands out in all its sturdiness in winter, the tree's massive feet and gray skin suggesting more elephant than plant. Without leaves to get in the way, you can see the majesty of an oak, its muscular arms outstretched like Atlas; you appreciate fully the golden fountain of a weeping willow's twigs cascading against a slate-colored sky. It's winter that reveals the Caliban personality of the Kentucky coffee tree (*Gymnocladus dioica),* whose elbowed branches seem to grasp outward uncouthly.

All by itself, a tree's shape can set the tone of a garden. Notice the aloofness of the upright European hornbeam (*Carpinus betulus* 'Columnaris' or 'Fastigiata'), whose nearly vertical, close-knit branches seem to say it wants to keep to itself. It has a formal quality, as does the fastigiate (narrowly upright) English oak (*Quercus robur* 'Fastigiata'). Compare the profiles, the sensual vase shape of the Zelkovas or an American elm (*Ulmus americana;* the cultivars 'Delaware II' and 'Washington' are both resistant to Dutch elm disease) with the trim fan-shaped canopy of a yellowwood *(Cladrastis lutea).* The shape of all shapes, certainly, is the weeping European beech (*Fagus sylvatica* 'Pendula'), whose branches start out horizontal and then turn toward the earth, forming a vast tent.

A wintertime inspection also spotlights another feature often overlooked among the distractions of the growing season: bark. Beautiful bark, surely, is the reason why every garden from zone 9 north should include a birch. Or better yet, two: a white-skinned variety such as the canoe or paper birch (*Betula papyrifera)* or the European white birch (*B. pendula),* as well as the more disease-resistant native river birch *(B. nigra)* or its cultivar (*B. n.* 'Heritage'), whose bark is pinkish white to salmon and peels handsomely. These birches really stand out, the color of their pale bark helping them advance in perspective; they become focal points. And no tree seems to go better with a snowy scene. Birches tend to have columnar shapes, and many have multiple trunks, which gives them an even more picturesque quality.

Kentucky Coffee Tree

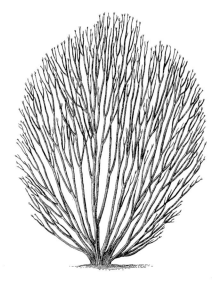

Upright European Hornbeam

Far left: The spreading, twisted branches of the Kentucky coffee tree (Gymnocladus dioica) *compose a loose canopy. At maturity, the tree can reach a height of 90 feet. Left: By contrast, the European hornbeam* Carpinus betulus *'Columnaris' has a dense multistem trunk that looks as if several branches are vying for the role of central leader. The slow-growing tree keeps its fanlike profile with little pruning.*

A number of trees have camouflage-pattern bark, which peels as the tree matures to leave behind varying splotches of gray, tan, and greenish gold. Among them are a number of small-scale trees: the Japanese stewartia and Kousa dogwood *(Cornus kousa),* both of which have decorative, multistemmed shapes, summer flowers, and colorful fall foliage to their credits, too. A number of cherry *(Prunus)* species have bark with a bronze or metallic sheen; the skin of the paperbark maple *(Acer griseum)* exfoliates as if it were made of cinnamon sticks. The moosewood *(Acer pensylvanicum),* an Eastern native maple, has white-striped green bark. Magnolias, beeches, yellowwood, and the Korean mountain ash are among those

River Birch

with smooth gray skin. And then the most outrageous bark of all: *A. palmatum* 'Sango-kaku,' the coral-bark Japanese maple, which, as its common name suggests, is hot-colored in winter.

A wintertime walk also highlights the importance of conifers, those evergreens that keep the green in the garden through the colder months. The choicest of them—like Japanese umbrella pine *(Sciadopitys verticillata),* weeping Alaska cedar *(Chamaecyparis nootkatensis* 'Pendula'), and *Abies concolor* or *A. koreana,* two exceptional firs, have beautiful shapes in their own right, and their needled mass provides a dramatic counterpoint to the deciduous trees' skeletal austerity.

Whatever trees you select for your garden, they must be more than just attractive. They must also be appropriate to the scale, soil, and light conditions of the intended site. You'll want them to please in every season, but that's why you make your selections in winter. It's easy for a tree to star in spring, when it's in flower, or fall, when the leaves turn brilliant colors. It's easy to like a tree in summer when you need the shade. Winter is the real test of arboreal character, and of the gardener's discernment.

The river birch (Betula nigra) *is as eye-catching in full leaf as it is when completely denuded of foliage. Whether allowed to grow multiple stems or pruned to have a single trunk, it provides an airy canopy that casts dappled shade in summer. In winter, the reddish brown of its young twigs and branches contrast with what is generally considered to be the whitest trunk of any birch species.*

Pruning Basics

Anticipation can be your most valuable pruning tool. By cutting twigs early in the life of the tree, you can direct its development into a strong, healthy pattern so that you won't have to remove large limbs later on. Pruning early and pruning small is much easier for you. It's also far less traumatic for the tree.

Success in developmental pruning depends on two things. Before you begin, you must first picture clearly how the mature tree should look. To do that, you must do a little research, and learn how that species of tree naturally develops. Then you balance the tree's natural inclinations with the needs of the site. A tree that will eventually shade a path, for example, should have no limbs lower than eight feet so that there will be no knocked heads.

The second essential for developmental pruning is continuity. Don't do much pruning at any one time, but prune regularly. Begin training each tree as soon as it has recovered from transplanting and resumed its growth, and thereafter prune twice a year: once during the tree's dormant season and again in summer. Each pruning session lasts only a few minutes, but because the effect is cumulative, it's important not to skip those few minutes.

Developmental Pruning

a. Upward Growth Establish a strong "leader," a central, upward-reaching shoot that emerges from the treetop to form the line of growth for the trunk. Often, you'll find two branches competing for this role. Choose the stronger one, and prune the other off at its base or cut it back to a side branch or bud to slow its growth.

b. Outward Growth Visualize where you wish the tree's canopy to begin; this may be 3 to 4 feet up the trunk in the case of a flowering dogwood, or 8 feet up for a shade tree such as a sugar maple. Prevent branches that sprout below your lower limit from developing into major limbs. As soon as they reach a length of 18 to 24 inches cut them back to 6 inches. When they've grown as thick as your little finger, cut them off at the base.

c. Branch Spacing Select the branches you wish to develop into main limbs. They should radiate evenly from the trunk like the steps of a spiral staircase; they should be spaced vertically at intervals equal to about 3 percent of the tree's mature height. On a tree expected to grow to a height of 50 feet, for example, major limbs should be spaced about $1^1/_2$ feet apart.

d. The Right Cut Before cutting a branch of any size, find the "collar," the swelling at the base of the branch where it emerges from the trunk. Cut just outside the collar at a slight angle, sloping down and away from the trunk.

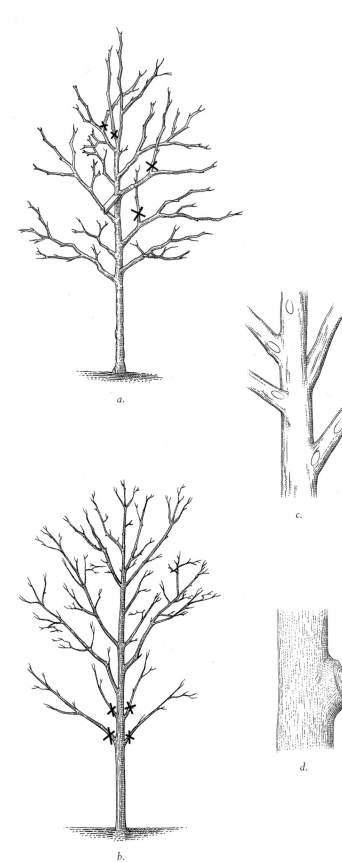

a.

c.

b.

d.

The Sensible Lawn

Lawns have developed an ugly reputation as ecological offenders, and with some justice. In their quest for the perfect green, American homeowners dump some sixty-seven million pounds of pesticides on their lawns every year, and more than a third of the average household's water bill is spent on landscape watering, the lion's share of this irrigation going to the lawn. The irrigation is heaviest where water is shortest, in the arid West and Southwest, and in many communities, lawn care is literally draining the rivers, aquifers, and reservoirs. Yet the fact is that grasses are naturally tough, self-sufficient plants; the problems with lawns are mostly of our own making.

More intelligent lawn care is an essential part of this situation's solution. Prepare the soil deeply, and dig in plenty of organic matter before you plant, to encourage deeper rooting; water deeply when you do irrigate, letting the turf dry out between waterings. During active growing seasons, fertilize the soil to replenish depleted nutrients. Feed it with either an organic lawn food, such as well-rotted manure, seaweed extract, or fish emulsion, or with a synthetic fertilizer. Should you select a synthetic product, make sure it contains slow-release nitrogen. Spread lime on the lawn only if a soil test indicates that your soil is markedly acidic (that is, if the pH level registers below 5.5). Above all, accustom yourself to the idea that a lawn doesn't have to be perfectly weed- and insect-free. Still, the best care in the world can't make a success of a lawn that is planted with the wrong grass.

Turf grass is not some anonymous, interchangeable green stuff. It is actually a group of many different species and varieties, each of which is adapted to a different climate, soils, and conditions. Different grasses have different strengths, too, so that the turf you plant for a high-traffic area should be different from the one you plant in a less-traveled part of the landscape. Generally, you plant a mix of grasses, because a diverse lawn is less susceptible to any one pest or problem. In any event, though, to achieve a healthy lawn for a reasonable investment of resources and effort, you must first identify the grasses adapted to your site and your uses.

Warm-Season vs. Cool-Season Grasses

All turf grasses belong to one of these categories, and the distinction is important, because it determines your planting schedule. Cool-season grasses are best planted in the late summer to early fall, as the heat subsides and the soil temperature begins to drop. Warm-season grasses, which need a higher germination temperature, should be planted in the late spring to early summer, as the soil is warming up.

Bermuda Grass is a warm-season grass that grows best in the South and Southwest. It spreads so quickly it can invade flower beds and won't tolerate shade. It is wear-resistant, however, withstanding regular foot traffic. It adapts to varying soil conditions, some drought, and salt air. "Common" Bermuda grass is drought-tolerant and

The commonest types of lawn mower are the reel or push mower, top, and the rotary or power mower, above. The reel mower has hardly changed since it was invented in 1830. Whichever type you use, leave clippings on the lawn, where they break down into fertilizer.

generally tougher; the "improved" or hybrid Bermuda grasses have a softer, finer texture and make a denser turf, but demand more care.

Buffalo Grass, a warm-season grass native to the Great Plains, is also popular in the South, thanks to its tolerance for heat and drought. It grows well on alkaline soils but does not flourish on sandy ones. It requires little irrigation, thriving naturally in areas where as little as 12 inches of rain falls annually. Improved cultivars are usually planted as sod, sprigs, or plugs; some of the older types may be started from seed, though the process is slow, and the resulting turf is of a poorer quality.

Fine Fescues are the most shade-tolerant of all lawn grasses and are usually a major element of "shady lawn" mixes for northern areas. They are cool-season grasses with a minimal requirement for fertilization and irrigation. Their tolerance for wear is only fair to poor. Fine fescues grow best where summers are cool.

Kentucky Bluegrass is a cool-season species that is the most popular lawn grass in the North. It germinates slowly but tolerates cold well, and heat moderately well. It has a relatively high need for water, which makes it a poor choice for areas of lower precipitation. Improved types tend to be more disease-resistant but also more dependent on fertilization and irrigation, and more intolerant of drought.

Perennial Ryegrass is a cool-season species that germinates quickly. Older varieties were considered coarse and unattractive, but newer "turf-types" have better texture and color. Often mixed with fine fescues and Kentucky bluegrass, perennial ryegrass is exceptionally resistant to wear and moderately tolerant of shade. Its need for fertilizer is low to medium, but it is a thirsty grass that needs abundant rainfall or regular irrigation. Best for coastal regions with moderate winters and cool, moist summers.

St. Augustine Grass is a warm-season turf popular in Florida and along the Gulf Coast, and well adapted to Hawaii. It is the most shade-tolerant of the warm-season grasses and can withstand high heat and humidity. Its tolerance for wear is poor, and it has a high need for water. It prefers neutral to alkaline soils.

Turf-Type Tall Fescues make a tough, attractive lawn ideal for play areas and athletic fields. They are more tolerant of heat than other cool-season grasses, and if given occasional deep waterings, they withstand drought exceptionally well. Moderately tolerant of shade, these fescues have a low to moderate need for fertilizer. Excellent for regions with mild winters and warm summers such as the upper South, lower Midwest and Mid-Atlantic states. Older varieties were tough, coarse, and prone to clumping; newer improved varieties offer finer texture and darker color.

Zoysia Grass, a warm-season turf, tolerates smog and pollution well. Slow to establish itself after planting, it eventually forms a very dense turf that is naturally resistant to invasion by weeds. Zoysia has a moderate tolerance for shade, good resistance to wear, and is exceptionally heat- and drought-tolerant. Its need for water is low, which makes it an excellent turf for areas with dry summers, such as the southeastern states, lower Midwest, and for southern California. Though fairly cold-tolerant, zoysia turns brown with the arrival of cool weather in the fall and doesn't regreen until mid to late spring in the north.

Top left: Bermuda is a warm-season grass that spreads quickly and grows well in the South. Center left: Perennial ryegrass often contains a natural insect repellent and is resistant to wear. Bottom left: St. Augustine is a popular sod grass in the Southeast.

Mowing Guide

It might be better to call it "pruning the grass." In fact, that is exactly what gardeners do as they push the mower around the yard, and perhaps if they thought of themselves as pruning while doing so, this fundamental chore might get the attention it deserves. For how a lawn is mowed decides how healthy it is. A lawn cut to the right height—this figure varies with the type of grass, the season, and the local climate—and at the right time will be healthier, thicker, and more resistant to weeds and bugs.

How often should you mow? Let the grass tell you that. Consult the table below to determine what is the ideal height for the type of turf you grow, and then mow whenever the grass rises up to one-third above the ideal figure. Keeping the grass at the right height is important because it en- courages stronger growth and deeper rooting, which makes your turf more resilient and better able to withstand drought. Our table expresses the ideal mowing heights as ranges; for example, the mowing range for tall fescues is 2 to 3 inches. Cut grass to the taller height when it is stressed, in particular when the weather is hot and dry.

Don't procrastinate: If you let the grass grow too long, you'll shock it when you do cut. Ideally, you shouldn't remove more than one-third of the leaf-blades with any one cutting—and keeping the clippings short means that you don't have to rake them up and re- move them. Instead, you can let them settle into the turf, where they'll decay and return their nutrients to the soil.

Grass	Ideal Mowing Height (in Inches)
Bermuda grass, common	$3/4$-$1\frac{1}{2}$
Bermuda grass, improved cultivars	$1/2$-1
Bluegrass, common	2-3
Bluegrass, improved cultivars	$1\frac{1}{2}$-$2\frac{1}{2}$
Buffalo grass	$1\frac{1}{2}$-2
Fescue, fine	1-$2\frac{1}{2}$
Fescue, turf-type tall	2-3
Ryegrass, perennial	1-2
St. Augustine grass	2-3
Zoysia	1-2

Gardening Strategies

Making nature your gardening partner is essential, even though sometimes, inevitably, it will be your adversary. Right from the start, you can enlist nature's help by choosing the plants that have adapted to your climate. The most convenient guide for making such choices is the Zones of Hardiness Map, which you'll find (with directions for its use) on page 128. And by consulting the short list of natural indicators on page 129, you can quickly learn to predict and understand the weather as your garden experiences it. • When winter settles in, however, nature often turns hostile. The protection you give your garden then can easily make the difference between life and death. • The most complicated interchanges with nature involve the gardener's relationship with the local wildlife. Developing the skills needed to coexist with all creatures great and small is one of the most important challenges you face.

In preparation for the drying winds, snow, and ice of the Connecticut winter, Martha likes to wrap broad-leaf evergreens such as boxwood with burlap. The debris of the planting beds is cut back, raked up, and removed, and a winter mulch is laid down to insulate the perennials and bulbs. Garden blankets also help secure plantings against harm from winter's blasts.

Zones of Hardiness Map

Selecting plants that prefer your climate is the best single guarantee of a trouble-free garden. Fortunately, there is a convenient and easy-to-use guide: the "Zones of Hardiness Map" (below) published by the United States Department of Agriculture.

This divides the United States and Canada into eleven zones. Because winter cold is, in most regions, the single greatest threat to plant survival, the zones are divided according to the average minimum temperature they experience locally.

Plant descriptions in nursery catalogs and labels typically refer to these hardiness zones to specify the areas in which any given species will thrive. A common garden peony, for example, may be listed as "hardy from zone 2 to 10," which means that it will flourish anywhere within the region bound by these two zones. Once you have identified the zone in which your garden is located, purchase only plants recommended as reliably hardy there.

This map divides the country into eleven zones—1 being the coldest and 11 the warmest—according to the average lowest annual temperature in each region (those minimum temperatures appear beside the color-coded zone key at right). The zones provide only general guidelines. Wind, humidity, summer sunshine, soil type, and other factors may also affect hardiness.

AVERAGE ANNUAL
MINIMUM TEMPERATURE

Zone		Temperature (°F)
1		Below -50
2a		-45 to -50
2b		-40 to -45
3a		-35 to -40
3b		-30 to -35
4a		-25 to -30
4b		-20 to -25
5a		-15 to -20
5b		-10 to -15
6a		-5 to -10
6b		0 to -5
7a		5 to 0
7b		10 to 5
8a		15 to 10
8b		20 to 15
9a		25 to 20
9b		30 to 25
10a		35 to 30
10b		40 to 35
11		40 and above

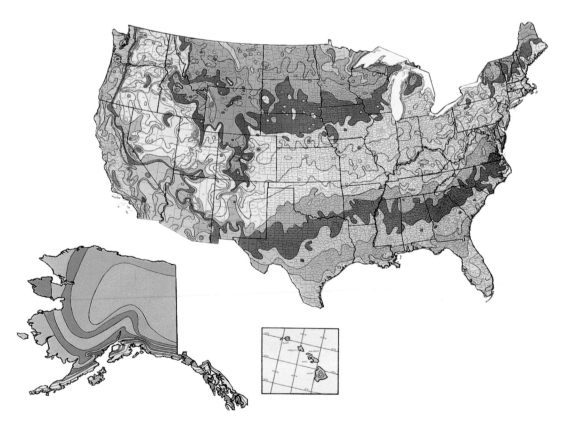

Weather

Climate (the pattern of precipitation, wind, sunshine, and other conditions that normally prevails in a region) must affect how you plan your garden, since it determines your zone. But weather—what's happening outside right now—should govern what you do in the garden day by day. It also tests the limits of your plants. Sheer heat, for example, typically troubles plants far less than heat combined with humidity, and temperature alone has less impact on plants than the rate at which the temperature changes. That's why, as a gardener, you should learn how to develop a weather forecast—one tailored to your plants. Here are some factors to look out for.

Frost: This is the worst threat in early spring as well as in fall. The basis for predicting frost is knowing when, on average, the first and last frosts of the year occur in your area. Any local nurseryman can tell you those dates—but they are only approximate. There are sure to be springs when a frost comes later, and autumns when

a frost comes earlier. How can you anticipate a late or early frost?

In the South, any weather that brings in northern air can be the signal; a "blue norther" is what Texans call the wind that sweeps down from Canada, causing temperatures to drop by as much as 50 degrees in a matter of hours. Northern gardeners, by contrast, should watch for a sudden clearing after a period of wind and overcast skies or rain. If the temperature plummets into the 40s by late evening, the air is still, the stars are visible, and there isn't any dew on the grass, then batten down the garden.

Covering garden beds with old sheets or plastic drop cloths can protect sensitive plants from a slight frost. Make sure the coverings reach all the way to the ground: The goal is to trap the heat that radiates from the earth. Clothespins that snap shut with springs are handy for fastening covers over shrubs such as roses. An alternative is to leave a sprinkler playing over your most vulnerable plants. The water droplets release heat as they cool, warming the plants below.

Wind: In most parts of the country, a southern or easterly wind is likely to bring precipitation within eighteen to twenty-four hours. A northern or west-

erly wind typically brings fair weather.

Wind can injure plants, particularly broad-leaved and other evergreens, by dehydrating them. The dry winds of a southwestern summer or a northern winter are particularly dangerous. You can protect dormant plants by wrapping them with burlap (see "Winterizing the Garden," page 132), but a more permanent solution is to erect a windbreak in the direction of the prevailing wind. A double hedge of compact, drought-resistant evergreen shrubs or trees will filter and slow the wind effectively, as will a louvered fence or a palisade of snow fencing. In general, a windbreak protects an area on its downwind side that extends ten times as far as the windbreak is tall.

Humidity: The easiest way to gauge atmospheric humidity is to look toward the horizon. Clear visibility of distant objects indicates low humidity. Haze indicates elevated humidity.

When combined with heat, high atmospheric humidity provides nearly ideal conditions for the breeding of fungal diseases. Wetting plant foliage increases the threat of infection even more. To irrigate during hot, humid weather, use a hose-end bubbler or a "leaky" soaker hose, and apply the water directly to the soil.

Some of the worst cool-season damage to plants is not from big snowstorms but from sudden frosts. And some of the best defenses against these frosts are the simplest: Bed sheets, draped over plants and held fast with clothespins, can keep light frost at bay.

Cold Frame This is a simple structure, really just a bottomless box with a transparent lid. Nevertheless, it provides a sheltered environment that allows for a twelve-month growing season.

Unlike a greenhouse or conservatory, a cold frame derives not only light but also its heat from the sun. The lid of the box is sloping, in part to shed rain and snow, but also because a lid angled toward the south admits maximum solar radiation. Generally, the bases of a cold frame's walls are sunken into the soil to insulate them.

So effective is this arrangement that on sunny days you must prop open a cold frame's lid to keep the temperature inside from rising above 75 degrees, the highest acceptable temperature for seedlings. The lid should be closed again in late afternoon to conserve the internal heat. On the coldest nights it is prudent to cover the frame with an old blanket or quilt to keep the temperature inside from dipping below the recommended low of 45 degrees.

A cold frame is the ideal spot to start seedlings in early spring—it furnishes not only bright light but also the cool nighttime temperatures that encourage sturdier growth. In late spring, a frame is also handy for hardening off tender seedlings. In summer, you can use it for starting seedlings of lettuces, cabbages, and other crops to be planted out later for a fall harvest.

After those seedlings have vacated the frame, it will accommodate root vegetables as well as cold-hardy brassicas and other greens, which extend the harvest season into December and beyond. Finally, in midwinter, the frame will furnish storage for potted crocus, tulip, and daffodil bulbs, keeping them dormant until it's time to bring them into the house for forcing.

You can buy a ready-to-assemble cold frame from many garden-supply catalogs, but building your own is easy and inexpensive. The model at left was assembled (as shown opposite) from an old, wood-frame storm window, simple hardware, and some boards, for about $150.

starting under glass

This cold frame, built from an old storm window and pine boards, is propped open with a dowel. Even on chilly days, it may be necessary to raise the lid to avoid overheating tender seedlings that may scorch when the temperature inside the frame is seventy-five degrees or higher. By midafternoon, the gardener may then lower the lid to trap and conserve heat for the cooler evening.

building a cold frame

1 A cold frame can be made with untreated pine boards and an old storm window. The larger the panes in the window the better (the dividers between panes block light). If necessary, reglaze the window using metal glazing points to hold panes in place and putty to seal them. Cut six 8-foot lengths of 2-by-12-inch lumber into 12 pieces: six 4-foot-5-inch boards for the front and back (you'll have one left over) and six 3-foot-4-inch boards for the sides. Two diagonal pieces will tilt the window at an ideal 35-degree angle.

2 This box is two boards high in front, three boards high in back. To assemble the bottom tier, drill galvanized screws into the boards at the four corners. Make the middle and top tiers the same way; attach them to the bottom with vertical wood strips screwed in the box's corners and sides as braces.

3 Once the frame is assembled, treat the frame with a nontoxic water-repellent stain, then let it dry for two days. Next, the frame may be painted—this one is green outside, to match the trim of the house, and white inside, to reflect light onto plants.

4 On a south-facing site away from the shade of trees and buildings, use a spade to dig a 12-inch hole with very straight edges. This depth will help to insulate the partially buried interior of the frame during both warm and cool growing seasons. (In very cold climates, earth may also be mounded up around the sides of the frame.)

5 After the hole is dug, it should be lined with several layers of weed-barrier fabric (available at many garden centers). Run the fabric up the sides of the hole and onto the soil surface around the frame, taking care to overlap pieces of fabric. The weight of the frame will hold the fabric in place.

6 Place the frame into the hole with the high side facing north. Backfill soil around the outside of the frame. Inside, lay a 4-inch layer of pea gravel for drainage; spread a 3-inch layer of builder's sand on top of the gravel to make a firm base for seed trays and pots. If you wish to use the frame itself as a seed-planting bed (e.g., for lettuce or spinach), shovel in a top layer of compost-enriched soil.

7 Attach the storm window to the frame with two small hinges on the inside of the high back wall. To keep the lid from blowing wide open in a stiff wind, attach a length of chain to one side of the window and to the side of the frame. Screw a metal bracket into the underside of the window frame so that a dowel can be inserted to prop open the lid for ventilation. Place pots of seedlings or bulbs inside the finished frame.

Winterizing the Garden

Putting the garden to bed in the fall is a two-stage job. It begins with a general cleanup right after the first killing frost and finishes with a tucking-in of vulnerable plants as cold weather settles in.

The goal of the cleanup is not just tidiness but also prevention. Any pests and diseases that afflict plants during the summer do not simply go away in the fall. Instead, they go dormant, leaving spores and eggs on the fallen leaves and withered stems. Gather any material from infested plants, such as leaves from blackspot-afflicted roses, and dispose of them. Compost other plant debris so that it won't become a haven for vermin.

Take time during your cleanup to cap all outdoor pots and urns. If left uncovered, water may fill them, and when this freezes, it will shatter terra-cotta or even concrete containers. Martha covers her containers with stainless-steel lids cut to fit. Aluminum, tin, and copper covers can be used as well; exterior-grade plywood is less attractive but effective all the same.

The second phase of winterization should focus on protecting plants from winter's four major threats: heaving, desiccation (drying), scalding, and breakage.

Heaving occurs when unseasonably warm weather temporarily thaws the frozen earth. When cold weather returns, the ground refreezes and the soil expands, heaving plants upward and dislodging them. Newly planted specimens are especially at risk. The best protection is to wait until the soil has frozen, and then insulate it to make sure it stays that way. Covering beds with a blanket of evergreen boughs (the post-holiday Christmas tree offers a handy supply) is the traditional insulation. Salt hay is equally effective, and unlike ordinary hay, it won't sow weed seeds. To keep it from blowing away, cover it with a crisscross of twine stretched between bamboo stakes.

Desiccation is the greatest wintertime threat to evergreen shrubs, especially the broad-leaved types such as rhododendrons and boxwoods. Winter winds draw water out of their foliage, and the roots cannot replace the lost moisture because the water in the soil is locked up as ice. The result can be browned leaves and needles or dead plants.

A loose wrap of burlap provides effective protection. Pound 2-by-2 stakes firmly into the ground on either side of the shrub. Then surround the plant with a skirt of 36-inch-wide burlap, stapling it to the stakes. Leave the top open—the shrub will need the ventilation on sunny days.

Young evergreen trees are more likely to have limbs broken by the weight of wet snow. Swaddling the trees with jute twine reduces the risk of such injuries. Wrap a strip of burlap around the base of the trunk to prevent chafing, and tie the twine around it. Then, carefully folding branches upward, use twine to bind the entire tree into a compact, upright bundle. A brief sortie during blizzards is also a wise precaution: Use a long-handled broom to push up heavy-laden branches, and shake off the accumulating snow.

Winter sunlight, weak as it is, can also damage woody plants, especially newly planted (and thin-barked) fruit trees. Though commonly called "scalding," what the sun actually does is warm the bark and the living wood below, so that the sudden plunge in air temperature at sunset causes them to crack and split. Wrapping the trunks of young trees at transplanting time is an easy form of prevention. Just wind a 4-inch-wide strip of burlap in a spiral up the trunk as far as the first branches, tie it on with twine, and leave it in place for the transplant's first two years in its new home.

Nature's version of a down comforter, snow is in fact more of a protector than a nemesis for gardeners. Snow can actually protect plants from the true danger of winter: cold, drying winds. Aside from its beauty, which highlights the garden's solid structure, a snow cover will provide plants needed moisture come springtime.

Animal Invaders

When it comes to pests, most gardeners settle for crisis management. They wait until a pest has become a problem before they take action. But that is simply too late. It is far easier to deter a pest than to evict it after it has found your garden to its taste.

Insects: Contrary to general opinion, it's fairly easy to coexist with the local insect population. Indeed, the smart gardener's goal isn't to have an insect-free garden—that's impossible. Instead, it makes sense to attract an assortment, so the insects compete with and prey on each other: Every segment of the bug population will serve as a check on the others' growth.

• Mix up your plantings to mix up the bugs. Most plant-eating insects are very specific in what they attack; commonly, a particular insect preys only on the plants of one genus or family. Planting a wide range of plants ensures that no one insect threatens more than a small part of the garden.

• Keep the targets small. Plant 100 petunias together, and you create a large and easy-to-find target for insects that favor petunias. Design your garden as a tapestry that weaves together small drifts of various kinds of plants and flowers, and you make it harder for insect pests to find the ones they favor.

• If a plant proves prone to insect damage, replace it with an alternative that your local nursery recommends as pest-resistant in your area.

• Have your soil tested for deficiencies of organic matter, nutrients, and minerals. Make sure you aren't watering and feeding too much or too little. A persistent pest infestation is likely a

pest barriers

Animal	Remedy
Gophers	To exclude these burrowing animals, plant in raised beds, lining the bottom and sides of the beds with light-gauge chicken wire or hardware cloth.
Rabbits	Exclude with fences made of 1-inch-mesh chicken wire. Set the fence in a 6-inch deep, 6-inch-wide trench, bending the wire mesh so that it lines the sides and bottom of the trench to stop burrowing. Refill trench with earth, and extend fence upward to stand 3 feet high. Commercial rabbit repellents provide some protection where fences are unsightly; mix the repellent with anti-transpirant, such as Wiltpruf, before spraying onto plants to keep it from washing off.
Woodchucks	See "Rabbits," above. Woodchucks climb as well as burrow, so attach the wire fencing to the outside of the posts, and leave fencing unfastened for the top 12 inches. When the woodchuck reaches this level, its weight will cause the fencing to flop outward and dump the intruder.
Deer	A single strand of electrified wire stretched 30 inches above the ground will exclude deer if you keep the wire smeared with peanut butter: The deer won't be able to resist a lick—accompanied by a jolt. An 8-foot-tall woven-wire fence is the standard deer barrier; two parallel 4-foot fences set 4 feet apart are also effective and less obtrusive. Black plastic deer netting (available at garden centers) blends in with the background and can be stretched from tree to tree or from posts.
Birds	Cover seed beds with floating row covers or with fine black plastic bird netting (sold at garden centers). Shroud berry bushes, grape arbors, etc. with bird netting, beginning 2 weeks before fruit ripens. Tying strips of tinsel to the netting and/or plants reinforces the deterrence.

symptom of poor maintenance—or misguided planting from the start. Once again, plant only species adapted to your site and climate.

Four-Legged Pests: They may be cuter than insects, but rabbits, woodchucks, gophers, and above all deer pose a far more serious threat to the garden. When hungry, these four-legged gluttons devour virtually any plant they find. And they'll return to eat the new growth as it emerges from the stumps, eventually killing even large shrubs and small trees. For a gardener, there is no coexisting with the mammalian nibblers and grazers. You have to lock them out.

No plant is totally deer-proof—deer will eat almost anything if they are hungry enough. However, there are some highly aromatic plants that seem to be not only unattractive to deer (as daffodils are), but downright repellent. Intermingle them with other plants, and these self-replenishing repellents should help to minimize the damage from deer.

deer-repellent plants

Catmint	*Nepeta* species	Perennial; hardy in zones 3 to 10, depending on the species. Well-drained soil; full sun.
Garlic	*Allium sativum*	Perennial; hardy in zones 5 to 10, depending on the variety; to north, grow as annual. Organic-rich, well-drained soil; full sun.
Honeybush	*Melianthus major*	Perennial; hardy in zones 8 to 10, zone 7 with winter protection. Moist, well-drained soil; full sun.
Lavender	*Lavandula* species; English lavender *(L. angustifolia)* is cold hardiest	Perennial; hardy in zones 5 to 10, depending on the species. Well-drained soil; full sun.
Mint	*Mentha* species	Perennial; hardy in zones 4 to 9. Moist, organic-rich soil; full sun to partial shade.
Sage	*Salvia* species; select types such as culinary sage *(S. officinalis)* with strongly aromatic foliage	Perennial; hardy in zones 4 to 10, depending on the species. Well-drained soil; full sun—some species tolerate partial shade.
Society garlic	*Tulbaghia viollacea*	Perennial; hardy in zones 8 to 10. Fertile, moist soil; full sun to partial shade.
Thyme	*Thymus* species	Perennial; hardy in zones 4 to 10, depending on the species. Well-drained soil; full sun.

Glossary

Amend: To incorporate an organic or mineral material such as compost, rock powder, sphagnum peat, fertilizer, or lime into the soil to enhance its fertility or structure, or adjust its pH.

As soon as the soil can be worked: A phrase commonly used to specify an early-spring sowing. In very early spring, your garden soil may still be frozen and so impossible to dig—to "work"—or, just after it has thawed, it is likely to be so wet that any attempt to dig it will only turn it into muck. When the soil has thawed and dried, squeeze a ball of it in your hand. If it shatters with the poke of a fingertip, then your soil is ready to be worked, and ready for the early sowings.

B&B: An abbreviation for "balled-and-burlapped." A B&B tree or shrub has been dug out of the ground with a ball of soil around its roots. This mass is then wrapped in burlap and tied to allow movement and transplanting.

Bare-root: A method for transplanting trees, shrubs, and perennials. The plant is dug up while dormant and the soil washed or shaken from its roots before it is packed for shipment.

Biennial: A plant, such as a pansy, that normally requires two years to germinate, grow, bloom, and set seed. Many such plants can be brought to flower in one growing season by start-ing the seeds indoors in late winter or very early spring.

Bolt: To suddenly sprout a stem and bear flowers, often in response to heat or drought. When lettuce, spinach, and other cool-season greens bolt, the leaves become tough and bitter and the crop must be replaced.

Broadcast: To scatter seeds over the soil, rather than planting them in rows or circular "hills."

Bulb (corm and rhizome): Though bulbs, corms, and rhizomes are similar in appearance and often used indis-criminately, the terms denote different types of underground storage struc-tures. A bulb (such as a daffodil or onion) is a bud enclosed in layers of leaf bases; a corm (crocus, gladiolus) is a swollen section of stem; a rhizome (bearded iris, daylily) is a horizontal stem. The exact type of storage organ determines the way in which the plant is divided or otherwise propagated.

Cane: The term traditionally used to describe the long, woody stems of roses and grapevines.

Cell pack: A lightweight tray of mold-ed fiber or, more often, plastic that is divided into many small sections like a muffin tin. Commonly used to hold potting mix for starting seedlings in a greenhouse or under lights indoors.

Corm: See Bulb.

Crown: The part of a plant where roots and stems meet, usually found at ground level.

Cultivar: Cultivated variety; a superior type of some plant species selected or bred artificially and maintained through inbred seed or by cloning (propagation by division, cuttings, grafting, etc.). Any plant name enclosed in single quotes (e.g., *Rosa* 'New Dawn') denotes a cultivar.

Cut back (and head back): To shorten a branch or stem, most often by pruning it to a point just above a bud or side shoot. Heading back involves removing the tip of a branch or stem to slow its growth or encourage bushiness.

Deadhead: To remove aging flowers before they set seed; a technique used to prolong a plant's blossoming, and to prevent plants from squandering energy on producing unwanted seeds.

Determinate: Determinate flowers are those types that bloom for a definite and restricted period, at approximately the same season every year. Indeterminate flowers are capable of blooming repeatedly throughout the growing season. When applied to vegetable crops, "determinate" describes those plants that stop increasing in size when they reach the flowering stage and bear flowers and fruits in a concentrated burst; indeterminate plants continue to increase in size after flowering begins, and bear flowers and fruit until the end of their growing season.

Die back: The death of a plant's stems or branches, proceeding from tip toward base. Commonly caused by frost, drought, or insect infestation.

Dormancy: A state of reduced activity into which plants retreat to survive seasons of cold, heat, or drought. Deciduous plants commonly shed leaves when entering dormancy.

Floating row cover: A row cover (see below) made of material so light that when loosely draped over a row, the plants themselves push it upward as they grow.

Foliar: Pertaining to a plant's foliage. Foliar diseases attack the leaves; foliar feedings are fertilizers applied to, and absorbed through, the leaves.

Genus: A group of closely related species. The first part of a plant's botanical name identifies its genus: *Phlox paniculata,* summer phlox, is a species in the *Phlox* genus. The plural of "genus" is "genera."

Germination: The beginning of growth for a seed; its first sprouting.

Hard (as in cut back or prune hard): Severely, as when cutting branches or trunks back by a half or more.

Hardy: Able to withstand the extremes of the local climate. Most often used to describe a plant's tolerance for cold, but may also denote tolerance for heat or drought.

Heirloom: Among gardeners, used to describe a plant that has been in cultivation for several (human) genera-tions. Heirloom plants often offer superior flavor and adaptation to the local climate, disease and pest resistance, as well as old-fashioned beauty.

Humus: A stable form of organic matter derived from the decay of plant and animal materials; a vital component of garden soils.

Hybrid: A plant produced by crossing two genetically dissimilar parents, typically plants of different species or even genera. Hybrids often demonstrate "hybrid vigor," growing faster and larger than either parent, while bearing more spectacular flowers and fruits.

Indeterminate: See Determinate.

NPK: Scientific shorthand for nitrogen, phosphorus, and potassium, the three nutrients used in greatest quantity by plants. The three-number formula (5-10-5, 20-20-20) on fertilizer labels identifies a product's NPK content.

Organic: Term used by gardeners to distinguish those sorts of soil amend-ments, fertilizers, and pesticides that derive from unprocessed natural products, as opposed to products chemically synthesized in a factory. Examples of organic products include manures, rock phosphate, and rotenone, an insecticide extracted from the roots of a South American plant; synthetics include ammonium nitrate, superphosphate, and malathion. Note that scientists define as organic anything containing certain types of carbon compounds, so that a chemist's organics actually include DDT.

Overwinter: To survive the winter season. A sensitive plant may need to be overwintered indoors; a hardy plant will overwinter in the garden.

Pathogen: A disease-causing organism, usually microscopic.

Perlite: A light, porous, granular material produced by heating and expanding volcanic rock. Water absorbent, but sterile (without plant nutrients), perlite is used to increase the drainage and improve the aeration of potting soils, and as a rooting medium for cuttings.

pH: A measure of acidity or alkalinity, in gardening usually applied to soils. pH may range from 0 to 14, with a pH below 7 indicating acidity, and a pH above 7 indicating alkalinity.

Pinch: To prune with the fingertips. The topmost bud of a shoot may be pinched off to promote branching.

Plant out: To transplant from a container, or from indoors, into the garden.

Rhizome: See Bulb.

Root ball: The mass of roots and soil exposed when a plant is slipped from its container or burlap covering or dug out of the ground for transplanting.

Root-bound: Having roots densely tangled or coiled around the root ball; a condition often seen in plants grown too long in a small container.

Rotate: To change the location each year (usually in a 3- to 4-year cycle) in which a particular vegetable crop is grown, to reduce the threat from soil-borne diseases.

Row cover: A light, permeable material, usually polypropylene or polyester, that is spread over rows of plants to protect them from insects and/or a light frost. Invaluable in the vegetable garden.

Self-sow: To bear seeds that germinate without assistance in the garden. A tendency to self-sow may be desirable, as with many kinds of wildflowers, but it can also turn a prolific flower or vegetable into a weed.

Shear: To clip with hedge shears, usually into a formal shape.

Species: The basic botanical unit, a group of similar individuals that interbreed freely. A plant's species is indicated by the second part of a botanical name: *Phlox paniculata* belongs to the *paniculata* species of the genus *Phlox*.

Sucker: Vigorous, vertical shoot originating from the roots or base of a trunk; suckers may also sprout from limbs or trunks cut back to a point below the lowermost side branch or bud, "to bare wood."

Thin: To pull out or cut off crowded seedlings so those remaining have adequate room for vigorous growth. In pruning, thinning involves the removal of stems and branches from a congested plant to enable more light and air to penetrate into the interior.

Till: To dig or cultivate soil to prepare it for planting.

Top dress: To spread fertilizer, compost, or manure over the surface of the soil around a growing plant in order to nourish it without disturbing the roots.

Tuber: A plant's swollen, underground storage organ, a modified stem or root with buds from which new shoots and roots may develop. Potatoes and dahlias both produce tubers.

Variegated: Having leaves that are marked, striped, or blotched with contrasting colors.

For terms explained in the preceding chapters, see the Index, page 142.

The Guide

Some of Martha's favorite mail-order sources are listed below. You may also find seeds, plants, tools, and other garden equipment through MARTHA STEWART EVERYDAY GARDEN, at KMART stores nationwide and through www.marthastewart.com.

Seeds

THE COOK'S GARDEN P.O. Box 5010, Hodges, SC 29653-5010; (800) 457-9703; www.cooksgarden.com. Kitchen garden essentials, plus flowers.

GARDEN CITY SEEDS 778 Highway 93 North, Room 13, Hamilton, MT 59840; (406) 961-4837; www.gardencityseeds.com. Edibles and flowers for cold climates.

JOHNNY'S SELECTED SEEDS 1 Foss Hill Road, RR 1 Box 2580, Albion, ME 04910; (207-437-4301; www.johnnyseeds.com. Wide range of every sort of seed.

NICHOLS GARDEN NURSERY 1190 North Pacific Highway, Albany, OR 97321-4580; (541) 928-9280; www.gardennursery.com. Herbs, vegetables, and flowers.

SHEPHERD'S GARDEN SEEDS 30 Irene Street, Torrington, CT 06790; (860) 482-3638; www.shepherdseeds.com. Edibles and many flowers.

SOUTHERN EXPOSURE SEED EXCHANGE P.O. Box 460, Mineral, VA 23117; (540) 894-9480.

www.southernexposure.com. Modern and old-fashioned vegetables and some flowers; Many heat-tolerant varieties.

Plants

ARBORVILLAGE P.O. Box 227, Holt, MO 64048; (816) 264-3911. Trees and shrubs.

ARENA ROSE CO. P.O. Box 3096, Paso Robles, CA 93447, (805) 227-4094, www.arenarose.com. Bare-root roses.

BRENT AND BECKY'S BULBS 7463 Heath Trail, Gloucester, VA 23061; (877) 661-2852; www.brentandbeckysbulbs.com. Both familiar and unusual bulbs.

CANYON CREEK NURSERY 3527 Dry Creek Road, Oroville, CA 95965; (530) 533-2166. www.canyoncreeknursery.com. Choice perennials.

COMPANION PLANTS 7247 N. Coolville Ridge Road, Athens, OH 45701; (740) 592-4643; www.frognet.net/companion_plants/. Extensive list of herbs.

FORESTFARM 990 Tetherow Road, Williams, OR 97544; (541) 846-7269; www.forestfarm.com. Trees, shrubs, and perennials.

HERONSWOOD NURSERY 7530 N.E. 288th Street, Kingston, WA 98346; (360) 297-4172. Unusual trees, shrubs, and perennials.

JOY CREEK NURSERY 20300 N.W. Watson Road, Scappoose, OR 97056; (503) 543-7474. Perennials and shrubs.

MCCLURE & ZIMMERMAN 108 W. Winnebago Street, P.O. Box 368, Friesland, WI, 53935; (800) 883-6998, www.mzbulb.com. Large selection of bulbs.

PICKERING NURSERIES 670 Kingston Road, Pickering, ON, Canada L1V 1A6; (905) 839-2111. Bare-root roses.

PLANT DELIGHTS 9241 Sauls Road, Raleigh, NC 27603; (919) 772-4794; www.plantdel.com. Perennials; hostas a specialty.

WELL-SWEEP HERB FARM 205 Mt. Bethel Road, Port Murray, NJ 07865; (908) 852-5390. Herbs.

Equipment

A.M. LEONARD, INC. P.O. Box 816, 241 Fox Drive, Piqua, OH 45356; (800) 543-8955; www.amleo.com. Tools and supplies; sells to home gardeners as well as to professionals.

GARDENER'S SUPPLY 128 Intervale Road, Burlington, VT 05401; (800) 955-3370; www.gardeners.com. Geared to the environmentally conscious.

WALT NICKE CO. P.O. Box 433, Topsfield, MA 01983; (800) 822-4114; www.gardentalk.com. Tools, gadgets, and supplies.

If you have enjoyed this book, please join us as a subscriber to MARTHA STEWART LIVING magazine. The annual subscription rate is $26 for ten issues. Call toll-free 800-999-6515, or visit our website, www.marthastewart.com.

Other books available in The Best of Martha Stewart Living series:

FAVORITE COMFORT FOODS

CRAFTS AND KEEPSAKES FOR THE HOLIDAYS
(Christmas with Martha Stewart Living, Volume 3)

ARRANGING FLOWERS

DESSERTS

DECORATING FOR THE HOLIDAYS
(Christmas with Martha Stewart Living, Volume 2)

DECORATING DETAILS

GREAT PARTIES

CHRISTMAS WITH MARTHA STEWART LIVING
(Volume 1)

GOOD THINGS

GREAT AMERICAN WREATHS

HOW TO DECORATE

HANDMADE CHRISTMAS

WHAT TO HAVE FOR DINNER

SPECIAL OCCASIONS

HOLIDAYS

Contributors

Special thanks to Garden Editor Margaret Roach, who has developed a distinctive voice in the gardening pages of MARTHA STEWART LIVING. *Thank you, too, to deputy editor Douglas Brenner, writer and gardener Thomas Christopher, executive editor Kathleen Hackett, art director Linda Kocur, copy editor Debra Puchalla, and design production senior associate Duane Stapp. Thank you to the editors, art directors, and garden experts whose insight and dedication contributed to the creation of this volume, notably: Andrew Beckman, John Beirne, James A. Bielaczyc, Claudia Bruno, Jeanine Colgan, Stacey Dietz, Stephen Drucker, James Dunlinson, Jamie Fedida, Dora Galitzki, Stephanie Garcia, Agnethe Glatved, Jill Groeber, Susan Heeger, Jennifer Hitchcox, Jim McKeever, Jim Nau, Eric A. Pike, Heidi Posner, Lee Reich, Scot Schy, Bill Shank, Gabrielle Chasin Simon, Lindsey Taylor, Emily Thacher-Renshaw, Gael Towey, Molly Tully, and Alison Vanek; and to everyone at the New York Botanical Garden, Wave Hill, Oxmoor House, Clarkson Potter, Satellite Graphics, and R.R. Donnelley and Sons. Finally, thank you to Martha, whose passion for the garden inspires us all.*

Photography

William Abranowicz
Pgs. back cover (bottom left), 56, 58 (middle), 75 (right), 124 (3)

Anthony Amos
Pgs. 19, 39 (3, right)

Michel Arnaud
Pg. 40

Christopher Baker
Pgs. 3, 14, 17, 68, 85, 90, 91, 92 (2), 103

Anita Calero
Pg. 38 (3)

Reed Davis
Pgs. 2, 29, 31 (7)

Todd Eberle
Pg. 95

Davies & Starr
Pg. 87

Richard Felber
Pgs. back cover (bottom center), 16, 62, 84, 102 (4)

Don Freeman
Pgs. 18, 116, 118

Michael P. Gadomski/Photo Researchers Inc.
Pg. 129

Dana Gallagher
Pg. 136

Gentl & Hyers
Pgs. 65 (left), 71

Lisa Hubbard
Pgs. 52 (4; middle and bottom left, top and bottom right) 64, 65 (right), 69 (2), 70 (top), 74 (2), 76

Thibault Jeanson
Pg. 58 (bottom)

Kit Latham
Pgs. front and back endpapers, 26, 27 (8), 70 (bottom), 73, 79, 80, 96 (2), 97 (2), 113

James Merrell
Pg. 8

Amy Neunsinger
Pgs. back cover (top left), 10, 66 (bottom)

Victoria Pearson
Pg. 114 (middle two)

Randy Plimpton
Pg. 126

Maria Robledo
Pgs. 66 (top), 77

David Sawyer
Pg. 15

Jason Schmidt
Pgs. 13, 39 (1; bottom left), 106, 108, 117 (top)

Victor Schrager
Pgs. 63, 72

Matthew Septimus
Pgs. back cover (top right), 22 (2), 23 (3), 24 (4), 32 (4), 37, 41, 44 (3), 45 (6), 49 (3), 50 (4), 51, 55 (7), 104 (4), 105 (4), 107, 115 (7), 117 (bottom 2), 123 (2)

Evan Sklar
Pgs. front cover, back cover (top center), 4, 20, 25, 34 (7), 39 (top left), 43 (3), 46, 47 (5), 58 (top), 59 (4), 60, 61 (7), 75 (left), 86, 93, 127, 130, 131 (7), 133

William Waldron
Pg. 33

Simon Watson
Pgs. 7, 99, 100, 101 (2)

Jonelle Weaver
Pgs. back cover (bottom right), 52 (2; top left, middle right)

Anna Williams
Pg. 5

Elizabeth Zeschin
Pg. 114 (top, bottom)

Illustrations

Harry Bates
Pgs. 120, 121, 122

Jack Molloy
Pgs. bookplate, 81, 109, 110, 111

Calligraphy

Elvis Swift
Pg. 81

Index